D1476293

MORNING
NOON
NIGHT

A WAY OF LIVING

SOHO HOUSE

Soho House 76 Dean Street, founded 2015

FOREWORD

Welcome to *Morning Noon Night*

I can't quite believe it, but SOHO HOUSE & CO turned 21 this year. Our first book, *Eat Drink Nap*, detailed the values we have held since the day we opened our door, and I've been astonished by how many of you went out and bought a copy. Since it was published, we've built Farmhouse on 100 acres of Oxfordshire countryside, transformed a former belt factory in Chicago, reimagined a 140-year-old palazzo in Istanbul, restored the shell of a listed Georgian building in Soho and launched our own collection of homeware, called Soho Home. And there's much more to come.

As we've gone from one club to 18, I'm often asked how we give each Soho House its own particular heart and soul, and still stay true to our founding values. My answer is always the same – we make spaces that take our members from morning, through noon and into the night in a relaxed home away from home. Whether it's designing our bedrooms, getting the lighting just so, or mixing the perfect nightcap, this is our way of living.

I hope you like it.

Nick.

NICK JONES

Alicante wallpaper
by Pintura Studio

'THINK IN THE MORNING.

ACT IN THE NOON. EAT IN THE EVENING.

SLEEP IN THE NIGHT'

William Blake, poet, painter and Soho local

CONTENTS

MORNING

PAGE 8

Starting the day the best way possible, from new coffee techniques
and tasty breakfasts to getting out in the garden

NOON

PAGE 92

Long lunches, afternoon lounging, plus our interior design team's
guide to making a new house into a home

NIGHT

PAGE 200

Creating dark spaces, cocktail recipes from around the Houses
and cafe-style, comforting dishes to cap off a big night out

RECIPE KEY: VEGAN ♡ VEGETARIAN Ⓥ

Soho House Berlin

MORNING

MORNINGS WITH US ARE PURPOSELY SIMPLE:
a good breakfast served in a great setting by someone
who cares that you are there. Whether you prefer
to spend the waking hours in your room or relaxing
around the House, there will always be hot coffee,
a daily paper and a comfortable place to sit.

Soho Farmhouse,
Oxfordshire

TIME FOR COFFEE

THE DAY RARELY BEGINS WITHOUT A CUP.
Coffee culture has exploded over the past decade,
and although there have been several new
contenders for our favourite style, the most
commonly requested coffee is still the good old
Italian cappuccino. We make more than one million
of them around the Houses every year.

HOW TO MAKE CHEMEX COFFEE

Don't be put off by the process – it's actually much easier than it looks. If you've gone to the effort of sourcing good-quality beans, a Chemex coffeemaker is the best way to let the flavour shine through. Here's how we do it.

1
—

Weigh 30g/1oz coffee beans and measure out 500ml/18fl oz of water
(the standard rule is 60g/2oz coffee per litre/1¾ pints of water).

2
—

Insert a paper filter into the Chemex, keeping the three-layered side facing the spout.

3
—

Pour hot water through the filter to rinse away any residue and warm
the glass. Without removing the filter, carefully pour away the water.

4
—

Using a coffee grinder, grind your beans to an even consistency before adding to the
filter. One rounded tablespoon of grounds will make one cup of medium-strength coffee.

5
—

Boil your water and use a small amount to wet the grounds.
Wait 30 seconds, allowing the coffee to bloom.

6
—

Slowly pour the remaining water over the coffee, using a circular motion to ensure an even soak.

7
—

Remove the filter and grounds carefully and discard.

8
—

Serve and savour.

FARMHOUSE SOURDOUGH BREAD

Makes 1 large loaf

Prep: 10 mins a day for 5 days | Cook: approx 5 hours with proofing time (V)

INGREDIENTS

**500g/1lb 2oz strong flour (plus up
to an additional 50g/1½oz to prevent
dough from sticking, if needed)
280g/10oz rye sourdough
starter (see below)
12g/2 teaspoons salt
15g/½oz treacle
130ml/4½fl oz dark ale
150ml/5fl oz water
Salted butter, to serve**

RYE SOURDOUGH STARTER

DAY 1

250g/9oz rye flour
250ml/8½fl oz warm water

Mix all together and leave in a closed container, like
a non-airtight sterilised jar, at room temperature.

DAY 2

250g/9oz of the mixture from day 1
125g/4½oz rye flour
125ml/4fl oz warm water

Mix all together and leave at room temperature in
a closed container. Repeat this process for 3 to 4 days
to develop a pleasant, sour smell. Adjust quantities
to improve consistency – add water if it's looking dry,
flour if it's looking wet. Use after a minimum of 5 days
feeding for a more established, flavourful starter.

METHOD

Mix the ingredients in a bowl. On a lightly floured surface,
knead the mixture for about 15 minutes until you have
a smooth, elastic dough. Form into a ball, place in a lightly
oiled bowl, cover and leave to rise somewhere warm. This
first proof can take from 40 minutes to 1½ hours, and the
loaf should double in size by the final proof.

Once ready, tip the risen dough onto a lightly oiled work
surface. 'Punch down' to remove air bubbles. Gently
stretch the front of the dough away from you and fold it
back on top of itself. Repeat with the back, left and right
sides. Place in the bowl, cover and leave to proof again.

After another 40 minutes, repeat the process and leave for
a further 40. Lightly punch down again, cover and leave
for 20 minutes. Next, roll the dough into a rugby ball-
shaped loaf and place in a flour-dusted banneton. Cover
and leave for 2 hours.

Preheat a roasting tin on the bottom shelf of the oven at
maximum temperature. Turn the loaf out onto a baking
tray, then place on the middle shelf. Pour a glass of water
into the roasting tin. Turn the temperature down to
225°C/425°F/gas mark 7. After 15 minutes, turn the bread
around. Another 15 minutes later, take it out and tap the
bottom. If the bread sounds hollow, it's cooked. If not,
remove from the baking tray and place directly on the
oven shelf to bake for a further 5-10 minutes.

Leave to cool for an hour before cutting and serve with
a wedge of salted butter.

Follow this recipe as a guide – remember all flours are different and many factors such as temperature or feeding
frequency can affect sourdough. Adjust quantities if needed to ensure the best consistency.

HOUSE
TIP

Chargrill the slices
before serving
for an added
touch of colour
and flavour

SALTED BUTTER

HOUSE
TIP

Don't add salt to
the water when
poaching eggs
– it breaks up
the egg white

AVOCADO TOAST AND POACHED EGGS

Serves 4 | Prep: 10 mins | Cook: 10 mins (V)

INGREDIENTS

4 ripe avocados, peeled,
stoned and cut into chunks
40g/1½oz spring
onions, finely sliced
15g/½oz coriander, leaves
removed and chopped
1 pinch dried chilli flakes
1 green jalapeño pepper,
finely chopped
80ml/3fl oz olive oil
50ml/1¾fl oz lime juice
Zest of 1 lime
Tabasco, to taste
Salt
8 medium eggs
White wine vinegar
4 large slices sourdough
Unsalted butter
Chives, finely chopped, to serve

METHOD

Put the avocado, spring onions, coriander, chilli flakes, jalapeño, olive oil, lime juice and zest in a bowl. Add a few drops of Tabasco, to taste, and a large pinch of salt. Mix roughly until evenly coated.

Now poach the eggs. Fill a large, shallow pan with water, adding 50ml/1¾fl oz white wine vinegar per litre/1¾ pints. Bring to a simmer. Break the eggs into separate ramekins, swirl the water around the pan with a whisk to create a vortex. Add the eggs one by one quite quickly, so they cook at the same time, moving them around a little so they don't stick to one another. Poach for about 3-4 minutes until the whites are soft and the yolks are runny.

Meanwhile, toast and butter the sourdough and place a generous spoonful of the avocado mixture on each slice. Remove the eggs from the pan with a slotted spoon and place on top. Season and serve. We like to add a sprinkle of finely chopped chives for added flavour.

SUPER GRAINS BOWL

Serves 1 large portion | Prep: 5 mins | Cook: 5-10 mins

INGREDIENTS

85g/3oz quinoa, cooked
85g/3oz farro, cooked
85g/3oz steel-cut oats, cooked
55ml/2fl oz unsweetened coconut milk
110ml/4fl oz unsweetened almond milk
½ tablespoon almond butter
1 teaspoon coconut flakes
½ teaspoon cacao nibs
½ teaspoon flax seeds
½ teaspoon chia seeds
10 blueberries
15 goji berries

METHOD

Combine the quinoa, farro, oats, coconut milk, almond milk
and almond butter in a pan, and simmer over a low heat until the liquid
has reduced by half and the porridge has thickened.

Pour into a bowl and garnish with the coconut flakes, cacao nibs,
seeds and berries to serve.

Soho Farmhouse

ATING

HOUSE
TIP

To achieve the best
texture, use soft
or silken tofu and
avoid overmixing
in the pan

SCRAMBLED TOFU WITH SPICY TOMATOES

Serves 2 | Prep: 15 mins | Cook: 15 mins Ⓥ

INGREDIENTS

2 garlic cloves, peeled and chopped
4 plum tomatoes, diced
1 teaspoon dried chilli
1 fresh chilli, finely chopped
1 small white onion, finely chopped
60g/2oz coconut oil
1 teaspoon lemon juice
1 tablespoon flax meal
1 packet tofu (around 400g/14oz)
2 teaspoons curry powder
1 yellow courgette, finely sliced
30ml/1fl oz extra virgin olive oil
A few fennel fronds, to serve

METHOD

To make the spicy tomatoes, fry the garlic until golden, add the tomatoes and chilli, and cook until thick. Pulse in a blender and sieve away any excess liquid.

Sweat the chopped onion in a pan with the coconut oil, transfer to a blender and puree with the lemon juice and flax meal.

Break up the tofu, soak in water for 15 minutes, then drain and toss with the curry powder.

Sauté the courgette in the olive oil until it starts to soften, then add the tofu along with the onion puree and warm gently.

Transfer to a plate and top with the spicy tomatoes.

Sprinkle with the fennel fronds to serve.

BAKED EGGS

Serves 2 | Prep: 10 mins | Cook: 45 mins

INGREDIENTS

40ml/1⅖fl oz olive oil
1 clove garlic, peeled and chopped
½ small white onion, peeled and chopped
1 red pepper, sliced and deseeded
90g/3oz chorizo, cut into approx 16 x 1cm/⅖in thick slices
10g/½oz tomato puree
400g/14oz can chopped tomatoes
150g/5oz cannellini beans from a can, drained
150ml/5fl oz water
Salt and pepper
4 eggs
Bread, for toasting (we recommend sourdough for this dish)

METHOD

In a heavy bottomed saucepan, heat the olive oil, then add the chopped garlic and onion.
Cook slowly to ensure the onion does not take on any colour.

Stir in the sliced pepper and chorizo. Fry for 10 minutes on a low heat with a lid on the saucepan,
stirring occasionally until the peppers are soft.

Add tomato puree and cook for a few minutes, stirring regularly. Pour in the chopped tomatoes,
cannellini beans, water, salt and pepper. Cook for 15 minutes, then remove from the heat.

Preheat the oven to 160°C/320°F/gas mark 3. Divide the tomato mixture between two ovenproof dishes.
In each dish, make two small wells in the sauce using a spoon, then crack an egg into each one. Place in the
oven until the eggs have just set (this should be around 10 minutes) and the sauce is bubbling.

Finish under the grill if need be, and serve with thick-cut slices of sourdough toast.

HOUSE
TIP

Make more tomato
mix than you need,
it freezes well and
goes perfectly
with cod

Meet the Makers

PADDOCK FARM

All the bacon we serve at Soho Farmhouse, our 100-acre property in the Oxfordshire countryside, is produced by local butchers (and brothers) Nick and Jon Francis. 'I started out working in theatre and Nick was a copywriter,' says Jon. 'We had two pigs at home in our paddock – hence our name. After Nick went on a butchery course, we butchered the pigs and cured the meat ourselves. and that's where it all started.' Together, they breed native Tamworth pigs a few miles down the road from Farmhouse and supply their award-winning pork to some of the best chefs in the country. More than 40 Michelin-star restaurants now serve their meat.

Tamworth pigs are one of the oldest breeds in the world. Descended from wild boars, they haven't been cross-bred like many British breeds. This gives the meat a unique flavour.

'It's always been about producing the tastiest pork. All our pigs start on grass and live outside in a stress-free environment'

NICK FRANCIS

HOUSE TIP

These pancakes can also be served with smoked salmon and poached eggs

SWEETCORN PANCAKES WITH AVOCADO AND BACON

Serves 4 | Prep: 20 mins | Cook: 30 mins

INGREDIENTS

500g/1lb 2oz sweetcorn from a can, drained
3 eggs
1 tablespoon parsley, chopped
125g/4½oz self-raising flour
3 teaspoons baking powder
½ teaspoon smoked paprika
Salt and pepper
80g/2¾oz spring onions, thinly sliced
Olive oil
2 avocados, peeled, stoned and quartered
8 rashers streaky bacon

METHOD

Place 300g/10½oz of sweetcorn, the eggs, parsley, flour, baking powder, paprika
and seasoning in a food processor and blitz until combined. Transfer
to a large bowl and stir in the remaining sweetcorn and the spring onion.

To make the pancakes, heat a little oil in a frying pan over a medium heat. One tablespoon of the
sweetcorn mixture makes one pancake. Simply scoop and place in the pan, forming the pancake
as you go. It doesn't need to look too neat. Cook for 2-3 minutes on each side until golden.

Season the avocado quarters, then griddle in a hot pan with a little olive oil until
lightly coloured. Place the bacon under the grill and cook until crispy.

Top the pancakes with the avocado and bacon to serve.

STEAK, EGGS AND POTATO HASH

Serves 4 | Prep: 15 mins | Cook: 40 mins

INGREDIENTS

6 large Desiree potatoes
4 litres/7 pints water
30g/1oz salt, plus extra for seasoning
Black pepper for seasoning
3 tablespoons clarified butter
Olive oil
1 tablespoon chives, chopped
1 tablespoon shallots, chopped
4 x 100g/3½oz minute steaks
4 eggs

METHOD

Place the potatoes, water and salt in a large pan and bring to a simmer. Cook for 5 minutes, then turn off the heat. Leave the potatoes to cool in the water, before removing and peeling off the skins. Finely grate and season with plenty of salt and pepper.

Preheat the oven to 180°C/350°F/gas mark 4. Add just enough clarified butter to the grated potatoes until they become moist, then tip onto a parchment-lined baking tray and spread out to create a 1cm/⅓in thick layer. Cover with another sheet of parchment and then flatten with an additional baking tray. This helps cook the top of the potatoes without having to flip them over. Cook for 25-30 minutes until the potatoes are almost golden. Remove the top tray and allow to cool.

Once cooled, cut the potato layer into quarters, then fry in a little oil until crispy all over. Place into a mixing bowl, season with salt and pepper, then break up with two forks to create texture. Mix in the chives and shallots.

Lightly oil and season the steaks, then place in a large sauté pan over a medium-high heat and cook for a minute on each side. Remove from the pan and leave the meat to rest for a minute.

Meanwhile, fry the eggs in a little butter. To serve, layer the hash, then the steak and top with a fried egg.

HOUSE
TIP
If you like your
Bloody Mary spicy,
try adding some
horseradish for
an added kick

HOW TO MAKE OUR HOUSE BLOODY MARY

Prep: 10 mins

INGREDIENTS

Makes 1

50ml/1¾fl oz Grey Goose vodka
100ml/3½fl oz tomato juice
25ml/5 teaspoons House
Spiced Mix (see below)
20ml/4 teaspoons lemon juice

To serve:

1 stick celery, trimmed
2 green olives
Lemon wedge
Freshly ground black pepper

Spiced Mix (Makes 6)

140ml/4¾fl oz Worcestershire sauce
2 teaspoons Tabasco
2 pinches ground pepper
2 pinches sea salt

Put the ingredients into a jug and stir. You can store any extra mix in the fridge.

METHOD

Mix all the ingredients together in a cocktail shaker with ice, rolling back and forth three times. Strain into a Collins glass with ice, and garnish with a trimmed celery stalk, two green olives, a lemon wedge and ground black pepper.

HOUSE PRESS BOTANICALS

An ideal remedy for the morning after the night before, the vitamins and nutrients in our cold-pressed Botanicals juices can give a much-needed boost. For a similar result at home, just blend the following ingredients. Each recipe makes a good-sized glass.

Prep: 10 mins per juice

ENERGY

3 medium-sized oranges, juiced
1 ripe mango, peeled and chopped
Seeds of 2 passion fruit
15g/½oz fresh ginger
¼ lime, juiced
5g/1 teaspoon cacao powder
1g/⅕ teaspoon maca extract

GLOW

100g/3½oz red grapes
Seeds of 2 pomegranates
1 guava, peeled and chopped
15g/½oz fresh ginger
1 lime, juiced
Rose water, to taste

REFRESH

200ml/7fl oz coconut water
⅛ honeydew melon
1 lime, juiced
1ml/¼ teaspoon vanilla extract
2ml/½ teaspoon camomile extract or
25ml/5 teaspoons very strong camomile tea

High Road House,
London

Soho Farmhouse

THE DAY AHEAD

WE GIVE GUESTS DEDICATED GETTING-READY SPACES
in our bedrooms. The time spent preparing for the day
ahead can be some of your most thoughtful and conversational.
Which is why we like to provide those who stay with us
room for thinking and talking – from comfy chairs in the
bathrooms to well-equipped, uncluttured dressing tables.

CHOOSING TILES

There's a bewildering choice when it comes to the style of
tiles you can choose for a bathroom or kitchen space. For us, the
building always dictates the final decision. In the concept rooms
for our future property in Downtown Los Angeles (pictured below),
we stayed true to the mid-century feel of the city by pairing
pale-blue mosaic tiles with polished brass hardware.

By Pataki Tiles
'We mixed these cracked glazed tiles with black marble and antique brass in the bathrooms at 76 Dean Street. They contrasted nicely.'

By American Restoration Tile
'Used on the bathroom floors of Ludlow House, they reflect the original tiles of the building when it was a gold-leaf factory.'

By Tabarka Studio
'Hand-painted tiles have lots of character, with their visible brush strokes and mottling. These are in the bathrooms at Babington.'

By Fired Earth
'We have these in a chequered pattern on the floor in Cowshed spa at Soho Farmhouse. They are handmade so feel pleasantly rustic.'

SOME OF OUR FAVOURITE TILES

Our interior designer Chelsea Nelson picks her favourite examples from around the Houses

By Art Antic
'Used for the bar in House Kitchen, Soho House Barcelona, these tiles are hand-glazed. I love the tactile 3D sunflower design.'

By Bert & May
'Graphic and fun, these hand-painted tiles really make an impact on the floor of Mandolin Mitte Roof in Soho House Berlin.'

By Design and Direct Source
'We are using these in the bathrooms for our new property in Downtown Los Angeles. I love how it works against brass.'

By Design and Direct Source
'A geometric style that's great in modern and traditional rooms. We use them in the showers of several cabins at Soho Farmhouse.'

Meet the Makers

BERT & MAY

What started off as a reclaimed-tile company in Spain, helmed by former barrister Lee Thornley, Bert & May has now evolved into a fully fledged specialist supplier of vintage-inspired tiles. Founded in 2013, many of its distinctive glazed tiles are featured around our Houses, most recently on the floor of Mandolin Mitte Roof in Soho House Berlin (pictured opposite).

The business is committed to using natural raw materials and pigments. Its tiles are handmade and hand-dyed using traditional techniques. It can take up to 10 minutes to make just one tile.

GET WASHED AND READY

Bathtubs and dressing tables take centre stage in many of our
larger bedrooms, providing a social atmosphere in which to get ready.
Pictured below, a concept room for Soho House Barcelona, and
opposite, one of our Large bedrooms in Soho House Istanbul,
a former palazzo in the heart of the city.

ROOM TO THINK

People often stay
at our Houses to get away
from it all, but we know
that from time to time you
have to get a little work
done. That's why, in lots of
our bedrooms, we factor
in a dedicated work space,
should you need to sit down
and get thinking.

RESTORING BUILDINGS

FARMHOUSE

THE ORIGINAL FARMHOUSE AT THE HEART OF OUR PROPERTY
in Oxfordshire first appeared on a local estate map in 1774. Before opening
Soho Farmhouse in September 2015, we spent a year and a half restoring the
Grade II-listed building, working hard to preserve all the original details.
At every step along the way, we treated it as if we were recreating a family
home full of personal touches and character. We fitted a large fireplace,
raised the roof to make space for more bedrooms and restored much
of the existing brickwork.

The building's exterior and interior underwent significant changes
to make the spaces work for larger gatherings.

IN THE LIVING ROOM, antiques are mixed with new and vintage pieces to complement the original features. We added a leather Chesterfield sofa as well as wallpaper designed by Robert Kime and cushions made from old Suzani textiles.

The kitchen and dining areas in the farmhouse feature vintage lampshades and taxidermy.
We took care to make the bedrooms feel simple and lived in, steering clear of clutter and fuss.

VINTAGE HUNTING

WE LIKE TO USE A MIX OF OLD AND NEW AROUND
the Houses in order to make each one feel different.
Siobahn O'Flaherty, one of our interior designers,
has been sourcing prize pieces from all over Europe for
almost a decade. Here, she shares just a few of the places
(and tactics) she uses to find the best in vintage.

KEMPTON PARK

The first market to be held on the grounds of this Surrey racecourse took place in 1979. It now has more than 700 stalls and is one of the largest twice-monthly markets in Britain, and a go-to destination for collectors and dealers. Be prepared to meet some characterful stallholders as you make your way around the site.

WHEN TO GO

The Sunbury Antiques Market at Kempton Park is open every second and last Tuesday of the month from 6.30am. 'I get there at six,' says Siobahn. 'Arrive any later and you'll miss out on the best finds. Dealers often get the first sweep and have the advantage of knowing the key vendors personally, so make sure you are in with a chance by running around quickly and making sharp decisions.' Go in summer when the weather's better and the French dealers come over.

BUYER'S TACTICS

If you are planning on buying multiple large items, hire a van. 'You don't want to be trying to get a courier to pick up your goods on the day – it's busy and stressful,' says Siobahn. It's free admission and free parking, and it will mean you can take that antique oak armoire home there and then. It's also a good idea to familiarise yourself with the market before you go, by downloading the site map from its website.

WHAT TO LOOK OUT FOR

The market sells everything from rare vintage textiles and taxidermy to Danish furniture, threadbare rugs and industrial lighting. It's a great place for filling up a new home or business.

HOUSE TIP

When market shopping always take a tape measure to check dimensions

ARDINGLY

The Ardingly International Antiques & Collectors Fair in West Sussex is the largest of its kind in South England and only around an hour from London. With over 1,700 stalls it's massive, so not ideal for those shy of spending the whole day scouring. Its increasing size has meant it now runs over two days and offers up a range of finds, from ceramics to iron radiators and everything in between.

WHEN TO GO

Dates vary but there are around three events a year. Check the website for details of the next fair and, as always, if you want to get the best pieces, you'll need to be willing to get there earl y. Gates open at a slightly more civilised hour of 9am.

BUYER'S TACTICS

There are cash machines on site but for convenience and speed, bring cash. 'You can still haggle, but not like you used to be able to,' says Siobahn. 'At most you'll get a tenner knocked off. The trick is that if you see something good, don't hesitate. Just buy it, and if it's big, ask the seller to put it aside and move on.' As the site is large, it's a good idea to jot down the phone number of the dealer so you can find them again afterwards.

WHAT TO LOOK OUT FOR

Furniture and larger items are outside, whereas inside there are smaller items like silver and jewellery. 'We pick up artwork and ornaments for the bedrooms here,' says Siobahn. 'I tend to take a shopping trolley with me for smaller items. The dealers laugh and say I look like a granny!'

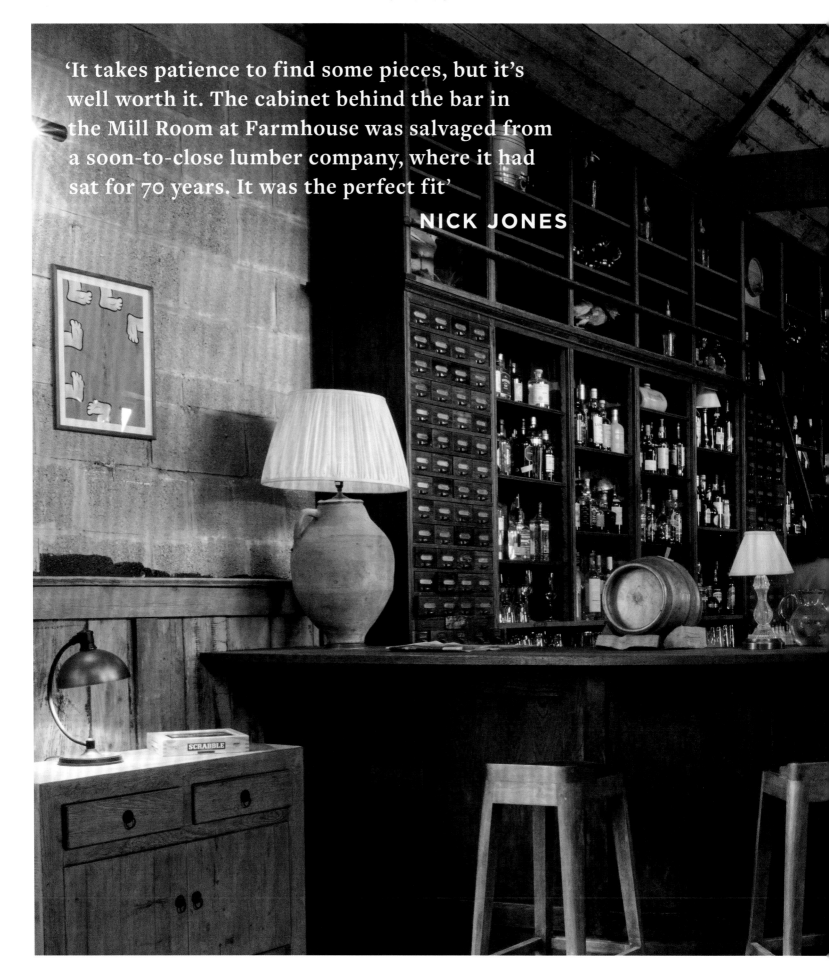

'It takes patience to find some pieces, but it's well worth it. The cabinet behind the bar in the Mill Room at Farmhouse was salvaged from a soon-to-close lumber company, where it had sat for 70 years. It was the perfect fit'

NICK JONES

MORENTZ

This 11,000sq m gallery, atelier and warehouse in the town of Waalwijk in the
Netherlands was a former shoe factory. It specialises in rare 20th-century design
– expect furniture and lighting for miles. Our interior design team often makes
a trip here to source key pieces for new restaurant openings and Houses. 'We used
them a lot for Berlin, Chicago and Istanbul,' says Siobahn. 'It's amazing, high-calibre
stuff.' Well worth a visit if you're after something that makes a statement,
like a one-off, mid-century chandelier.

WHEN TO GO

Anyone can go to the showroom. It's open Monday to Saturday from 10am until 6pm.

BUYER'S TACTICS

Don't expect flea-market prices here. This is a high-end store aimed at individuals looking
for top-drawer, designer vintage, with quality restoration and upholstery services.

WHAT TO LOOK OUT FOR

Beautifully preserved mid-century design. 'The giant chandelier we used as the centrepiece
at Cafe Monico on London's Shaftesbury Avenue was found here,' says Siobahn. 'They also curate
large quantities of the same item, so if you are opening a restaurant or hotel, it's the ideal place.'

**HOUSE
TIP**

Don't worry about
getting it home:
Morentz will help
with shipping to
anywhere in
the world

RESTORING BUILDINGS

76 DEAN STREET

OUR NEWEST LONDON CLUB, ON SOHO'S HISTORIC DEAN STREET,
was originally built in 1732. After it was destroyed by a fire in 2009,
SOHO HOUSE & CO purchased the Grade II-listed Georgian townhouse and
spent 18 months restoring it to its former glory. We added an extension to the
back of the original structure, along with a roof terrace and a courtyard.

The 2009 fire devastated the property. Following a series of emergency works
to stabilise the building, a design team was drafted in to remodel the site.

THE BLUE ROOM
features a restored Georgian
fireplace, vintage marble
cladding and 100-year-
old pine wood floors. The
wall panelling, dados and
cornicing were replicated
in line with the building's
Grade II listing.

The main staircase has an 18th-century mural that took more than 12 months to restore (above right).
A smaller original Georgian staircase was also reinstated and bespoke furniture now fills all four floors.

The Boathouse,
Soho Farmhouse

THE ENGLISH GARDEN

GARDENS NEVER LOOK MORE BEAUTIFUL THAN FIRST THING
in the morning, right after the sun has risen. Post-breakfast, there's
nowhere better to stroll, coffee in hand and witness nature waking up.
The classic English garden is rambling, busy and full of charm.
At Babington House and Soho Farmhouse, we've used large pots of
quintessentially English flowers such as chives (pictured opposite)
and daisies to root the gardens entirely in the landscape.

A planter at Soho Farmhouse features hydrangeas, roses, scabiosa and Silver Dollar eucalyptus.

MAKING AN ENTRANCE

We try to pay as much attention to the details on the outside
as the design on the inside. From pathways and entrances
to doorways and doorknobs, we believe the journey to a place
is often as important as the place itself.

Opposite: the lavender pathway to the farmhouse. Above: the cobbled
exterior and the Cabin doorway at Babington House, Somerset.

COFFEE SPOT

Everyone loves a quiet corner. At Babington House, fig trees and a pair of large terracotta pots create the perfect place to enjoy a morning coffee and take in the views of the Victorian walled garden.

HOUSE TIP

Climbers such as honeysuckle or clematis will soften man-made structures

HOW TO CREATE AN ENGLISH BORDER

Jo Whitfield-Jones, landscape gardener at Soho Farmhouse,
gives her tips on the best plants and shrubs to create
a classic yet modern English garden.

1
—

Start with a blank canvas. Prepare the ground, clear it of weeds,
fork it over and add grit where needed.

2
—

When choosing your plants, include up to 30 per cent evergreens, plus perennial
plants that need little maintenance, such as catmints, salvias and irises.

3
—

Plant a few varieties in large groups rather than lots of different ones.

4
—

Using evergreen grasses will make any garden seem more contemporary
– snowy woodrush is one of my favourites.

5
—

Bulbs, like snowdrops and tulips, extend the flowering season and create
a firework-like effect; as one variety dies, another one blooms.

6
—

For an elegantly English feel, include lavender and roses. If space is tight,
climbing roses work well, are relatively fast-growing and highly effective for covering
blank external walls. Wisteria is a more dramatic option.

7
—

Apply a good layer of mushroom compost over all flowerbeds to retain moisture
and keep the weeds down.

The Victorian walled
garden at Babington
House is overlooked by
the Cowshed spa and
three split-level bedrooms.

HOUSE VASES

The right flowers add colour and charm to a room. At Soho House, we prefer pretty, loose arrangements that look like they've come straight from the garden. Vases such as jugs, glass bottles or old cans can be found anywhere – from antiques shops to car boot sales. Here are a few of our favourites.

TABLE ARRANGEMENTS

Filling your home with freshly cut flowers can seem like a luxury, but just a few well-chosen blooms can enliven and transform a space. We prefer simple, laid-back displays rather than anything too fussy.

H O U

1: ALLIUM

Easy to grow and dramatic, the allium is part of the onion family. It flowers in late spring, grows tall and looks elegant in borders.

2: ROSEHIP

We use this bright red fruit in autumnal flower arrangements, but it is also used when making herbal tea, bread, wine and marmalade.

3: CHERRY BLOSSOM

The national flower of Japan blooms from late February to early May. A few branches can make a beautiful, simple display.

4: THISTLE

The prickles on Scotland's national flower are designed to fend off herbivores, but they are worth grappling with for floral displays.

F L O

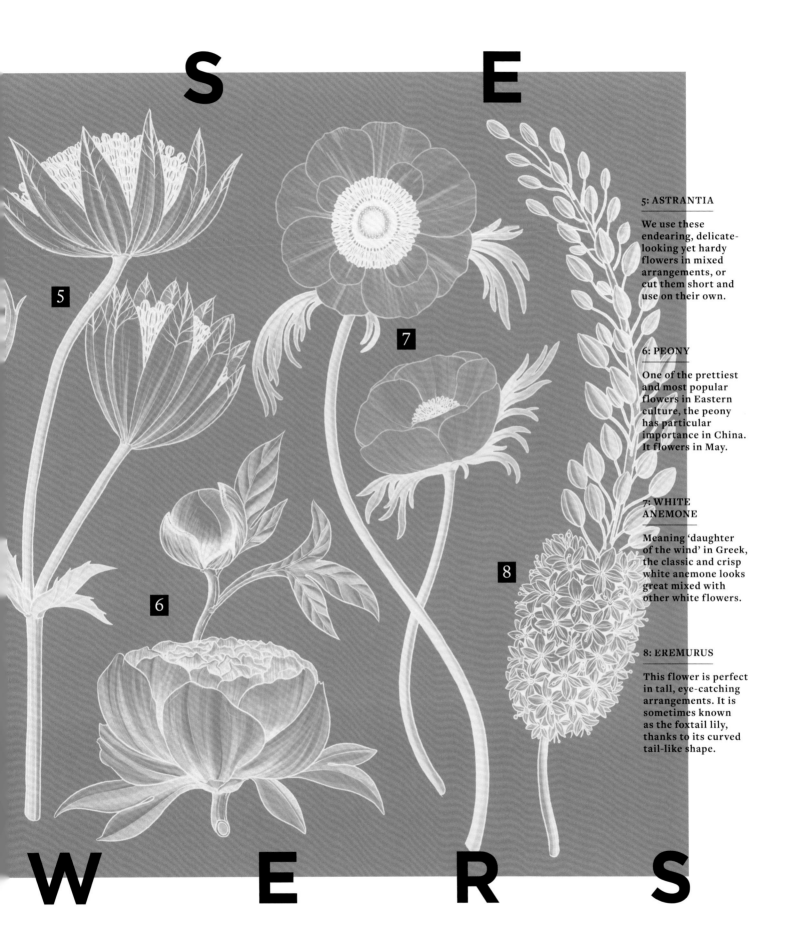

S E

5: ASTRANTIA

We use these endearing, delicate-looking yet hardy flowers in mixed arrangements, or cut them short and use on their own.

6: PEONY

One of the prettiest and most popular flowers in Eastern culture, the peony has particular importance in China. It flowers in May.

7: WHITE ANEMONE

Meaning 'daughter of the wind' in Greek, the classic and crisp white anemone looks great mixed with other white flowers.

8: EREMURUS

This flower is perfect in tall, eye-catching arrangements. It is sometimes known as the foxtail lily, thanks to its curved tail-like shape.

W E R S

Cookhouse,
Soho Farmhouse

NOON

NO MATTER WHERE IN THE WORLD WE LIVE, when the clock nears 12 and we feel the rumble in our bellies, it's time to think about lunch. It's one of our three favourite meals of the day.

LUNCH AT MANDOLIN

INSPIRED BY THE TAVERNAS OF AEGEAN COASTAL TOWNS,
the original Mandolin Bistro was opened by Turkey-born Ahmet Erkaya
and Greek-Canadian Anastasia Koutsioukis in Miami in 2009. It
was one of Nick Jones' favourite places to eat during the development
of Soho Beach House, sowing the seeds of a happy partnership.
There are now Mandolin restaurants at our Miami, Istanbul, Shoreditch
and Berlin Houses – with more to come.

MEZE DIPS

TOMATO WALNUT
Prep: 10 mins ♡ V

INGREDIENTS

2 large ripe beef tomatoes
30g/1oz toasted walnuts,
coarsely chopped
30g/1oz spring onions, chopped
1 garlic clove, peeled and chopped
1 tablespoon pomegranate molasses
1-2 tablespoons extra virgin olive oil
1 tablespoon chopped parsley
Salt and pepper, to taste

METHOD

Cut and mash the tomatoes and
drain any excess liquid through
a colander. Fold in the remaining
ingredients and serve.

HUMMUS
Cook: 30 mins (for garlic)
Prep: 10 mins ♡ V

INGREDIENTS

3 whole garlic cloves, peeled
50ml/1½fl oz extra virgin olive oil
Salt, to taste
200g/7oz cooked chickpeas
1 tablespoon lemon juice
40g/1½oz tahini
Cumin, to taste

METHOD

Preheat the oven to 180°C/350°F/
gas mark 4. Toss the garlic in the
olive oil and salt. Bake until tender
(about 30 minutes) and remove from
the oven. Place all the ingredients
in a food processor and puree until
smooth. Serve.

PINK SULTAN
Cook: 1 hr (for beetroot)
Prep: 10 mins V

INGREDIENTS

4 large red beetroot
112ml/3¾fl oz extra virgin olive oil
Salt and pepper, to taste
60g/2oz labneh (Greek yoghurt)
Small handful fresh mint
2 tablespoons lemon juice

METHOD

Preheat the oven to 180°C/350°F/gas
mark 4. Toss the whole beetroot in olive
oil with some salt and pepper. Tip into
a roasting tin, cover with foil and cook
for about 1 hour or until tender. Set
aside to cool. Peel the beetroot and
grate on the coarse side of a box
grater into a bowl. Mix in the rest of
the ingredients and serve.

HOUSE
TIP

We like to serve with freshly baked Turkish pide, or toasted pita bread for a quick and easy alternative

MUSSELS

Serves 4 | Prep: 10 mins | Cook: 5-10 mins

INGREDIENTS

60 mussels
6 garlic cloves, finely chopped
2 tablespoons olive oil
1 tablespoon dried oregano
500ml/18fl oz dry white wine
Juice of 2 lemons
2 tablespoons unsalted butter
Flat leaf parsley, chopped, to serve
1 lemon, cut into 4 wedges, to serve

METHOD

Place a pot big enough to hold the mussels over a medium heat, and fry the garlic in the olive oil, cooking for about 2 minutes until slightly browned.

Add the mussels and oregano to the pot, along with the white wine. Turn the heat up to high and cover.

After 3 minutes, the mussels will start to open. Add lemon juice and butter, and continue cooking until all the mussels have opened (discard any that don't) and the butter has melted into the sauce.

Divide the mussels between four large bowls, pour over the juices from the pan, sprinkle with chopped parsley and serve with lemon wedges.

VILLAGE SALAD

Serves 4 as a side dish | Prep: 10 mins Ⓥ

INGREDIENTS

4-6 ripe tomatoes, coarsely cut
1 cucumber, peeled, deseeded and sliced
¼ small red onion, thinly sliced
(white onion can also be used)
½ green pepper, thinly sliced
1 handful of capers
Sea salt
1 slab of feta cheese
1 handful marinated, pitted Kalamata olives
2 pinches dried oregano
1 pinch cracked pepper
Extra virgin olive oil
Red wine vinegar

METHOD

Toss the tomatoes, cucumber, onion, pepper and capers together in
a large serving bowl. Add ½ pinch of salt (remember you are adding
feta cheese on top, which is already very salty).

Arrange the feta and olives on top of the salad – presenting the feta as a
whole slab is our contemporary twist. Sprinkle with oregano and pepper.

Dress the salad with a generous amount of olive oil
and a splash of red wine vinegar, and serve.

MEET
ANASTASIA

'Ahmet and I founded Mandolin in 2009. We were living in New York
when a holiday to Miami inspired a dream that we couldn't shake off.
We moved into a 1940s Florida bungalow, restored it to its original glory
and opened our Aegean bistro, inspired by the food we'd grown up eating.
I hope you enjoy recreating our signature dishes in your own home.'

'FOOD ALLOWS
US TO EXPLORE
CULTURES AND
MEET PEOPLE.
WE LOVE TO
ENTERTAIN
– WORKING
WITH SOHO
HOUSE JUST
MAKES SENSE'

ANASTASIA
KOUTSIOUKIS

GRILLED PRAWNS

Serves 4 | Prep: 25 mins | Cook: 8-10 mins

INGREDIENTS

12 tiger prawns, heads and shells intact
1 teaspoon paprika
1 teaspoon dried oregano
6 tablespoons extra virgin olive oil
Sea salt
1 lemon, cut into 4 wedges, to serve

METHOD

Using a sharp pair of scissors, carefully cut through the shell of each prawn from the backside, starting at the tail and going through the body, stopping before the head and exposing the vein.

Carefully remove the vein and rinse the prawns in cold water, keeping the shells and heads intact and essentially 'butterflying' them.

Place ½ teaspoon of paprika, ½ teaspoon of oregano and the olive oil in a bowl, and mix well. Pour over the prawns and leave to marinate for 15 minutes.

In the meantime, preheat the grill to medium. Season the prawns with sea salt and grill for roughly 4 minutes each side, moving them as necessary so the shells don't burn.

Continue grilling until the flesh is opaque. Divide the prawns between four plates and sprinkle with the rest of the paprika and oregano. Drizzle with olive oil and serve with lemon wedges.

HOUSE
TIP

If you're short on time,
ask your fishmonger to
butterfly the prawns
and remove the
veins for you

HOUSE
TIP

Always buy from a
busy fishmonger and
look for clarity in the
eyes of the fish – it
signals freshness

GRILLED WHOLE MEDITERRANEAN SEA BASS

Serves 4 | Prep: 10 mins | Cook: approx 15 mins

INGREDIENTS

1 large Mediterranean sea
bass, filleted (approximately
600g-900g/1½-2lbs)
2 tablespoons salt
1 tablespoon dried oregano
½ tablespoon black pepper
½ lemon, grilled, to serve

FOR THE SAUCE:

3 tablespoons extra virgin
olive oil
1 tablespoon freshly
squeezed lemon juice
1 pinch salt, oregano
and pepper

METHOD

Let the fish sit in the fridge for a couple
of hours before you cook it. This will
allow the fish to firm up and keep it
together while grilling. Bring the grill
pan or BBQ to a medium heat. Take the
fish out of the fridge, pat dry with a paper
towel and lightly oil all over.

Place the salt, oregano and pepper
in a bowl, and mix together. Sprinkle
evenly over the whole fish. This will
create a crust on the skin after grilling.

Grease the grill pan or BBQ with olive
oil and place the fish on it. Cook for 7-8
minutes, then flip the fish over and cook
for 4-5 minutes on the other side. Don't
cook it for any longer or it will dry out.

Place the fish on a large plate to rest,
and prepare the sauce in a small bowl.
Using a fork, whip the olive oil with the
lemon juice and a pinch of salt, oregano
and cracked pepper, beating the mixture
until it thickens.

Garnish the dish with half a grilled
lemon and serve the sauce in a ramekin
on the side.

HOUSE
TIP

The fish is ready
to be turned
over when it lifts
away from the
grill easily

MARINATED GRILLED OCTOPUS

Serves 4 | Prep: 10 mins | Cook: 1 hr 30 mins

INGREDIENTS

1 large frozen octopus, defrosted (approximately 1.5kg/3½lbs)
240ml/8½fl oz extra virgin olive oil, plus a drizzle to serve
115ml/3¾fl oz red wine vinegar
2 tablespoons dried oregano
2 dried bay leaves
1 tablespoon salt
1 tablespoon whole black peppercorns
Lemon wedges, to serve

FOR THE MARINADE:

125ml/4½fl oz red wine vinegar
250ml/9fl oz extra virgin olive oil
1 tablespoon oregano

METHOD

Place all the ingredients in a pot, cover and simmer over a low heat for
1-1½ hours. The defrosted octopus should release enough liquid to cook in,
but if not, fill the pan with enough water to just cover the ingredients.
When tender, remove the octopus and leave to cool.

Whisk all the marinade ingredients in a bowl and set aside.

When the octopus has cooled, use a sharp knife to remove the tentacles
and discard the head. Gently toss the tentacles in the marinade and
refrigerate overnight. The next day, grill the octopus until warmed through
and serve with a drizzle of olive oil and a lemon wedge.

DISH OF THE DAY
Every Mandolin restaurant makes a focal point of Anastasia Koutsioukis' ceramics collection. Right: pieces from Mandolin Mitte Roof, Soho House Berlin.

ANASTASIA'S COLOURFUL KITCHEN

Bright, patterned crockery is all part of the Mandolin experience, where the plates and bowls are so pretty they make eating off them a delight. Here, Mandolin's founder reveals her tips and sources for recreating the look at home.

1
—

Start by investing in classic white porcelain plates that will mix well with bright colours and patterns. This can apply to glassware, too.

2
—

Pick your favourite colour and build a collection around it. There are no rules, just as long as there's a common link between the patterns. I always make sure there's a shade of blue in the patterns I choose, so when I use them all for a large dinner, they work well together.

3
—

Add texture to your table top with wood, raffia, stone, marble, glass and brass. Even if you are creating a monochrome setting, the different textures add interest.

4
—

Travel is my biggest source of inspiration. I scout flea markets, local artisans and vintage shops on every trip. People have been designing pottery and crockery for centuries and every culture, tribe or village has its own distinctive style or pattern.

5
—

Use things in unexpected ways. I love to serve soup or desserts in vintage cups or copper coups. Use items that reflect the culture of the food you're serving. Your table tells the story and sets the tone of the night.

HOW TO GROW YOUR OWN VEGETABLES

Anna Greenland, head gardener at Soho Farmhouse, shares her tips for starting your own organic garden.

1
—

Good soil is everything, and healthy soil means healthy plants. Do a soil test to find out what type you have – the ideal pH is around six or seven. Based on that, you can add manure or compost to create good soil structure. If you have particularly acidic soil, you might want to add lime.

2
—

Think about what you like to eat and what you'd like to grow. Look into heritage varieties, which have adapted over time, are resilient and have good flavour. Herbs and edible flowers are nice additions and attract bees.

3
—

Plan a new garden in autumn and early winter so that you are ready to sew and plant in February or March. A small greenhouse can give you a head start bringing up seedlings before you replant them outdoors.

4
—

Don't sew everything at once. Little and often is best, so your crops grow in succession. Kale and chard are good choices because you can keep cropping them throughout the season.

5
—

Watch out for pests. Some of these are specific to certain vegetable families, so research can make sure you're primed and ready before any problems arise. Organic gardening is much more work because you're not using pesticides.

6
—

You need to think about crop rotation. You shouldn't grow the same vegetables in the same place season after season, so always be thinking about what's next. When one crop is finished, another needs to be ready to go in.

HOME-

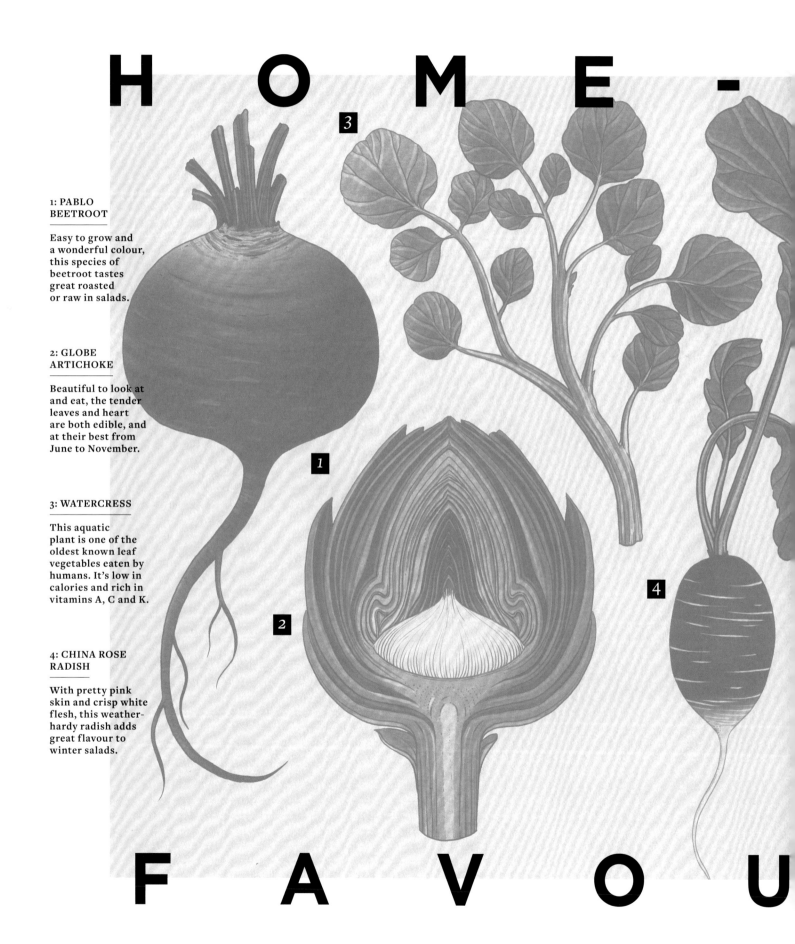

1: PABLO BEETROOT

Easy to grow and a wonderful colour, this species of beetroot tastes great roasted or raw in salads.

2: GLOBE ARTICHOKE

Beautiful to look at and eat, the tender leaves and heart are both edible, and at their best from June to November.

3: WATERCRESS

This aquatic plant is one of the oldest known leaf vegetables eaten by humans. It's low in calories and rich in vitamins A, C and K.

4: CHINA ROSE RADISH

With pretty pink skin and crisp white flesh, this weather-hardy radish adds great flavour to winter salads.

FAVOU

GROWN

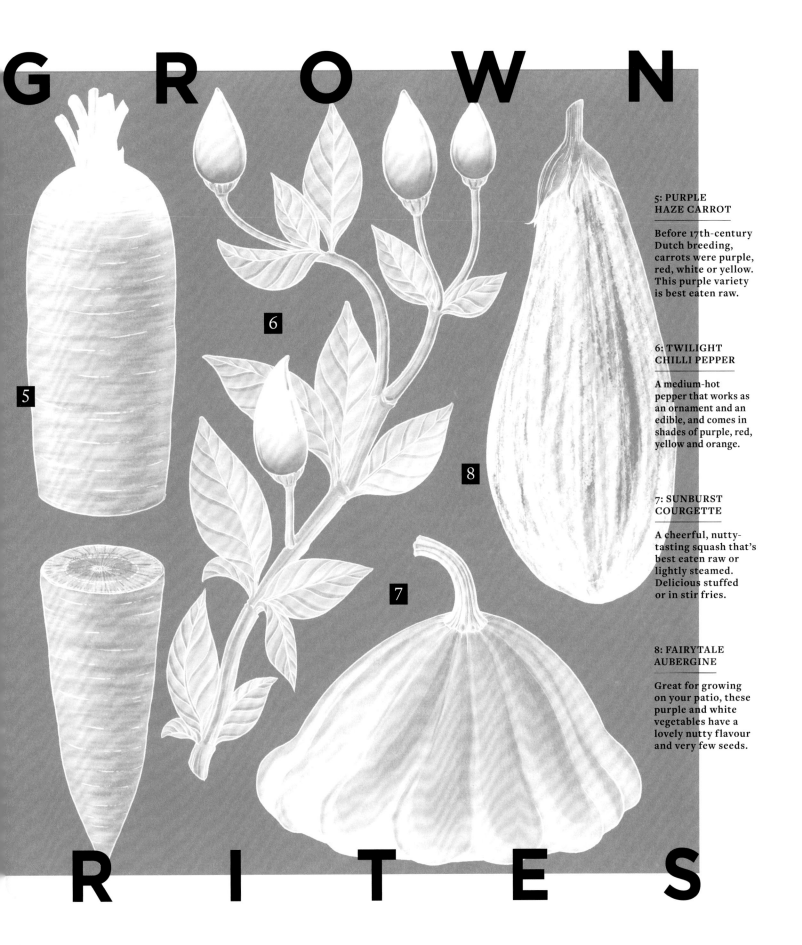

5

6

8

7

5: PURPLE HAZE CARROT

Before 17th-century Dutch breeding, carrots were purple, red, white or yellow. This purple variety is best eaten raw.

6: TWILIGHT CHILLI PEPPER

A medium-hot pepper that works as an ornament and an edible, and comes in shades of purple, red, yellow and orange.

7: SUNBURST COURGETTE

A cheerful, nutty-tasting squash that's best eaten raw or lightly steamed. Delicious stuffed or in stir fries.

8: FAIRYTALE AUBERGINE

Great for growing on your patio, these purple and white vegetables have a lovely nutty flavour and very few seeds.

RITES

The Playroom,
Soho House Istanbul

MOVE TO THE LOUNGE

IT'S ONE OF OUR FAVOURITE THINGS TO DO ON ANY GIVEN
afternoon: sink into a comfortable seat after a long, lazy lunch.
We're often asked what makes the perfect lounging spot.
Simple – a great sofa. That's why no matter what House
you happen to be in, you'll find plenty of them: expansive,
plump and difficult to get up from (sorry about that).

THE ART OF D

Soho House Chicago

DOING NOTHING

PICKING PATTERNS FOR LIVING SPACES

Choosing and committing to a pattern isn't easy. Here, our interior designer, Vicky Charles, provides some pointers.

1
—

Use a fabric you love to inspire where you go with any given space. The pattern can then define the room: the colours you pull out from it, the mix of furniture, the era or style you want to emulate.

2
—

We often use the pattern in a rug, fabric or wallpaper to influence the room we are designing. Stripes are a good entry-level way of using pattern, they feel like less of a commitment but still add variety and texture.

3
—

Use different scales. Don't overwhelm the space with different patterns of the same size. If the furniture has dominant large patterns, then the curtains need tighter, more delicate ones and vice versa.

4
—

I love to use patterned fabric headboards in bedrooms. If it's bold, go softer elsewhere in the room.

5
—

Choose paint colours after choosing patterns. The pattern you use will help you decide the colours that complement or contrast.

6
—

A good upholsterer will lay out pattern properly, centralising large motifs and matching the patterns on larger items.

Tribu by Stark
'I like how modern and mid-century this is. It's used on the benches at Nava in Soho House West Hollywood.'

Paisley by Carleton V
'The Chicago building was so masculine, I loved the idea of highlighting that by using more feminine pattern and colour.'

Palm by Great Outdoors
'We used this in the garden in West Hollywood and in Pen Yen at Farmhouse.'

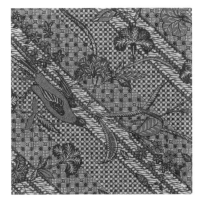

Java by Michael S Smith
'We covered our Spoon Sofa with this fabric in The Allis, Chicago.'

VICKY'S FAVOURITE PATTERNS

Our interior designer picks out her favourite fabrics from around the Houses

Bukhara by Lewis & Wood
'A vivid pattern that looks perfect pleated on lampshades.'

Oasis by Pintura Studio
'This was a custom watermelon colour we originally used for some of the sofas in Soho Beach House Miami.'

Bohemian Tapestry by Mulberry Home
'We used this on the dining chairs at Farmhouse. It's elegant but worn.'

Pienza by Clarence House
'An amazing mix of colours in a bold pattern that has a glamorous feel for a sofa in West Hollywood.'

'It's important to buy the pieces you like and not concern yourself too much with whether things will match or go. Sometimes great things happen when you mix it all together'

VICKY CHARLES, INTERIOR DESIGNER

A PAIR OF CHAIRS

We use matching chairs all around the Houses, from reception
rooms and restaurants to bedrooms and bathrooms. Using two
chairs in the same style rather than one gives balance and symmetry.
They add punctuation and look particularly good if used to divide
wider rooms. Mid-century designers were especially good at
creating chairs that worked well side by side, with elegant
wooden arms and curved legs.

BED FELLOWS

Two small tub chairs at the foot of a bed create an inviting
opportunity to relax, in Soho Beach House Miami.

SOMETHING BRIGHT

Two yellow mid-century chairs sit side by side in the Drawing Room of Soho House Chicago, helping to break up the space and create a focal point.

HOUSE
TIP

Use a leather wax
to feed the hide,
so it won't dry
out and crack

LOOKING AFTER LEATHER CHAIRS

A regular sight at many of our clubs, battered through years of use and all the better for it, leather club chairs really take some beating. Here, our interior designer Siobahn O'Flaherty gives some advice for picking and preserving your favourite chairs.

OLD NOT NEW

'We always choose vintage leather over new for the Houses, because you just can't buy that sort of character in a new piece,' says Siobahn. Cracks and scrapes are all part of the charm, but if they are too worn, vintage-looking new leathers can be used to recover arms. Refresh the seat pad by recovering in velvet or heavy wool.

CHECK IT OVER

'Big cracks are a sign that the leather has dried up,' says Siobahn. 'Avoid buying these, no matter how much you like the way the chair looks. It will just keep tearing.' It's also a good idea to check the springs are in good working order as these are not worth replacing further down the line. 'Check the frame is stable, too,' says Siobahn.

FIND A BALANCE

'Nick loves to find a balance between leather and textiles in every House,' says Siobahn. 'There is definitely such a thing as too much leather. Be sure to limit yourself by only using one or two hidebound pieces per room.'

INVEST AND CARE

'Leather is expensive. If you are going to spend the money, invest in great quality. We use a few key suppliers we trust,' says Siobahn. A favourite with the team is Brownrigg Interiors in Gloucestershire, but good finds do come up on eBay.

The Allis,
Soho House Chicago

AFTERNOON TEA AT THE ALLIS

THE ALLIS, OUR CAFE IN THE LOBBY OF SOHO HOUSE
Chicago, occupies the vaulted room of a historic former
belt factory. Every afternoon, we offer a spread of
finger sandwiches, tea, cakes and scones, served
on our own range of floral Burleigh pottery.

HOW TO MAKE THE PERFECT CUP OF TEA

A cup of tea is one of life's simple pleasures, but getting it right is another thing altogether. With this in mind, our suppliers at Canton Tea Co take us through the art of brewing tea, which, if done properly, should be refreshing and smooth with a clean flavour and satisfying aftertaste. Bear in mind that not all tea should be brewed in the same way, but for a cup of classic English breakfast, follow these steps.

STEP 1
The ideal ratio for Canton Tea Co's English breakfast blend is 8g/¼oz loose tea per 250ml/8½fl oz water. Loose leaf tea is best because it allows the tea to move around in the pot and infuse. Teabags are not all bad, and there is definitely a time and a place for them. Pyramid-shaped bags with full leaf tea are the type to go for.

STEP 2
Use fresh filtered water to fill your kettle and never reboil – it changes the water's mineral content and will affect the flavour of the tea. The ideal temperature for English breakfast tea is 95°C/203°F. Try to catch the kettle just before it boils.

STEP 3
Allow the tea to steep for 3-4 minutes (4-5 minutes if you're adding milk). If you like stronger tea, add more tea leaves rather than brewing it for longer.

STEP 4
Pour the tea. Whether the milk goes in first or last is a matter of personal preference, but adding it first results in a creamier flavour because the milk emulsifies when the tea is poured in. Adding the milk last allows you to pour exactly to your taste. If there is any tea left in the pot, pour it into a jug to keep it from brewing too long.

HOUSE TIP
Most good-quality tea leaves can be used twice

HOUSE TIP

Use a decorating comb to create even lines in the frosting. Start with the sides and then move to the top

DEVIL'S FOOD CAKE

Makes 1 x 20cm/8in cake; serves 8 | Prep: 15 mins | Cook: 50 mins Ⓥ

INGREDIENTS

170ml/6fl oz water
42g/1½oz cocoa powder
260g/9oz sugar
225g/8oz flour
1⅛ teaspoons salt
1⅔ teaspoons baking soda
170ml/5¾fl oz buttermilk
125ml/4½fl oz vegetable oil
3 eggs

FOR THE CHOCOLATE FROSTING:

270g/9½oz unsalted butter
270g/9½oz dark (70 per cent) or bittersweet chocolate
2 teaspoons vanilla extract
450g/1lb icing sugar
300ml/11fl oz sour cream

METHOD

To make the frosting, melt the butter and chocolate in a bowl over a pan of hot water, then pour into the bowl of an electric mixer fitted with the whisk. Add the vanilla extract and the icing sugar, and whisk on low speed until smooth. Add half the sour cream and keep mixing. It might look curdled at this point, but don't worry. Add the remaining sour cream and mix until smooth. Place in a container and leave to set.

To make the cake, start by bringing the water to a boil. Add the cocoa powder while whisking by hand and bring back to the boil. Remove from the heat. Sift the dry ingredients into the bowl of an electric mixer. In a separate bowl, combine the buttermilk, oil and eggs, and whisk until smooth. Add this to the dry ingredients and mix until smooth. Add the liquid cocoa mixture and combine. Pour the batter into two oiled 20cm/8in round cake tins and bake at 170°C/325°F/gas mark 3 for 25-30 minutes, or until a skewer inserted into the centre comes out clean. Allow to cool.

Spread two scoops of frosting on one of the chocolate cakes. Place the other cake on top and leave to set in the fridge. Once the cake is set, cover with the remaining frosting.

LEMON TART

Makes 1 x 20cm/8in tart or 6 x 10cm/4in tarts | Prep: 15 mins | Cook: 1 hr, plus chilling time Ⓥ

INGREDIENTS

FOR THE SWEET PASTRY:

150g/5oz unsalted butter,
at room temperature
70g/2½oz icing sugar
1 egg yolk
170g/1oz plain flour
½ tablespoon vanilla extract

FOR THE LEMON CURD:

75ml/2½fl oz freshly
squeezed lemon juice
Finely grated zest
of 1 lemon
1 egg, plus 3 yolks
140g/4⅘oz caster sugar
40g/1½oz unsalted
cold butter, cubed
Blueberries, to garnish

METHOD

First make the pastry bases. Using an electric mixer, beat the butter and icing sugar in a bowl on medium speed until smooth. Add the egg yolk until combined, then add the flour and vanilla extract to form a dough. Wrap in cling film and chill in the fridge overnight.

Roll out the dough to a thickness of about 6mm/¼in for large tarts and 3mm/⅛in for small tarts. Line the tart tins with the dough. Trim the sides and prick gently with a fork to prevent air bubbles. Let them rest in the fridge for 1 hour, or until the pastry feels hard. Preheat the oven to 180°C/350°F/gas mark 4. Bake for 15 minutes for the larger tarts or 10 minutes for the small ones until golden brown. Leave to cool.

To make the lemon curd, combine the lemon juice, zest, egg, yolks and sugar in a glass bowl and place over a pan of hot water. Slowly cook over a low heat, whisking occasionally, until the mixture becomes very thick. Remove from the heat and add the cold butter. Mix until all the butter has melted.

Pass the lemon curd through a fine sieve into a bowl and cover with cling film. Place in the fridge to set for 4 hours. Once cold, pipe into the baked tart cases and garnish with blueberries.

Meet the Makers

BURLEIGH

The craftsmen behind our unique range of floral crockery have been honing their skills for more than 150 years. 'We still apply pattern using a 300-year-old technique involving hand-engraved copper plates and tissue paper,' says Steven Moore, creative director at Burleigh. We visit their headquarters in Middleport, Staffordshire, which opened in 1889, to watch what goes into every cup, plate and saucer.

Burleigh's floral prints are transferred onto glaze tissue, then cut to size and fitted to the ceramic piece by hand. Due to this labour-intensive process, each one feels unique.

CHOCOLATE CHIP COOKIES

Makes 24 large cookies | Prep: 20 mins | Cook: 20 mins Ⓥ

INGREDIENTS

225g/8oz unsalted butter, at room temperature
1 tablespoon vanilla extract
210g/7⅖oz light brown sugar
200g/7oz caster sugar
2 eggs
420g/15oz plain flour
1½ teaspoons salt
¾ teaspoon baking soda
150g/5oz dark chocolate chips (preferably 65 per cent)
Maldon sea salt, to taste

METHOD

Preheat the oven to 180°C/350°F/gas mark 4. Place the butter, vanilla extract and sugars in a bowl and, using an electric mixer, cream the ingredients together until smooth, light and fluffy. Add the eggs one at a time until mixed in.

In a separate bowl, combine the flour, salt and baking soda and gradually add to the mixture. Mix until just combined. Add the chocolate chips and mix roughly. Do not overmix.

Separate the dough into 24 pieces and lay them out on greased or parchment-lined baking trays, making sure you leave enough room between them to spread. Sprinkle each with a pinch of Maldon sea salt. Bake in the oven for 15 minutes or until the cookies are golden brown.

HOUSE TIP

Refrigerate or freeze any spare dough for another batch, or use raw mixed with ice cream

The Allis,
Soho House Chicago

RESTORING BUILDINGS

SOHO HOUSE CHICAGO

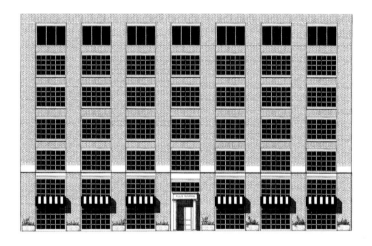

SOHO HOUSE CHICAGO OPENED IN 2014 IN A BUILDING
that was once the Chicago Belting Company. The six-storey concrete
structure was originally built in 1907 by the Allis family, who set up shop
in the West Loop area of the city in order to be close to the meatpackers,
who provided them with the animal hides needed to make their industrial
leather belts. As always, our goal was to celebrate the unique features
of the site, restoring the iconic chicken-wire, glass windows and taking
inspiration from the metal latticework for the House logo.

Above: the building in its original state. Below: the Classical Revival door surround and ionic columns were preserved (right), as were parts of the original vintage windows (left).

A LARGE GREEN VELVET banquette snakes along one wall of the Drawing Room. A lot of our members come to the House alone, so it made sense to have seating that suited both small and large groups equally.

Above: Art Deco-style shelving divides the lobby (left); bespoke butterfly painting by British artist Damien Hirst entitled 'Chicago' (right). Below, right: custom-made lights hang in the main Club Bar.

OUTSIDE SPACE

It's good to get outside. Over the years we've built everything from an outdoor pool on a roof overlooking the iconic Chicago skyline (pictured below), to a crispy duck restaurant in the eaves of a one-time funeral parlour on New York's Lower East Side (Ludlow House, pictured opposite). We always try to make the most of our blue-sky spaces, so you can make the most of them, too.

Pen Yen, a Japanese grill restaurant in the Boathouse at Soho Farmhouse, has 12ft retractable windows with views over the boating lake.

SIX THINGS TO CONSIDER WITH OUTSIDE SPACES

Scarlett Supple, the interior designer who helped create the communal spaces at Soho Farmhouse, gives her pointers on how to tackle outdoor rooms.

1
—

Start by creating a focal point. Clever seating layouts can help, as can a wood burner, creating a cosy atmosphere from spring through to winter.

2
—

Lighting is crucial. Use outdoor lanterns and decorative wall lights to create a good atmosphere. Strings of festoon lights are a cheap and stylish way to liven up a courtyard or garden.

3
—

Hard-wearing and durable fabrics will survive rain showers and mucky foot prints. Most modern outdoor furniture is designed to let rain run off and to air-dry quickly. Don't be tempted to move or store them, that's when they get marked or mouldy.

4
—

Create a covered space in case of high winds or rain. It also means you can use indoor furniture outside. At Farmhouse we use sofas and ottomans covered in robust wool kilim rugs.

5
—

Flowers and potted plants are a lovely decorative way to break up a space and create individual zones.

6
—

Vintage furniture and eclectic pots add character and depth to your space.

Farmyard,
Soho Farmhouse

TAKING THE IN

SIDE OUTSIDE

DRESSING
THE
OUTDOORS

We spend years finding the right locations and properties.
One thing always wins us over: the view. A case in point is
Little Beach House Malibu, which enjoys 180-degree views
over the Pacific Ocean and offers the chance to spot some of
the local wildlife, including sea otters, dolphins and grey whales.

Opposite: all-weather chairs at Little Beach House Malibu. Above: sunloungers at Soho House Berlin.
Below: leather chairs at Soho House West Hollywood (left); seating at Soho Farmhouse (right).

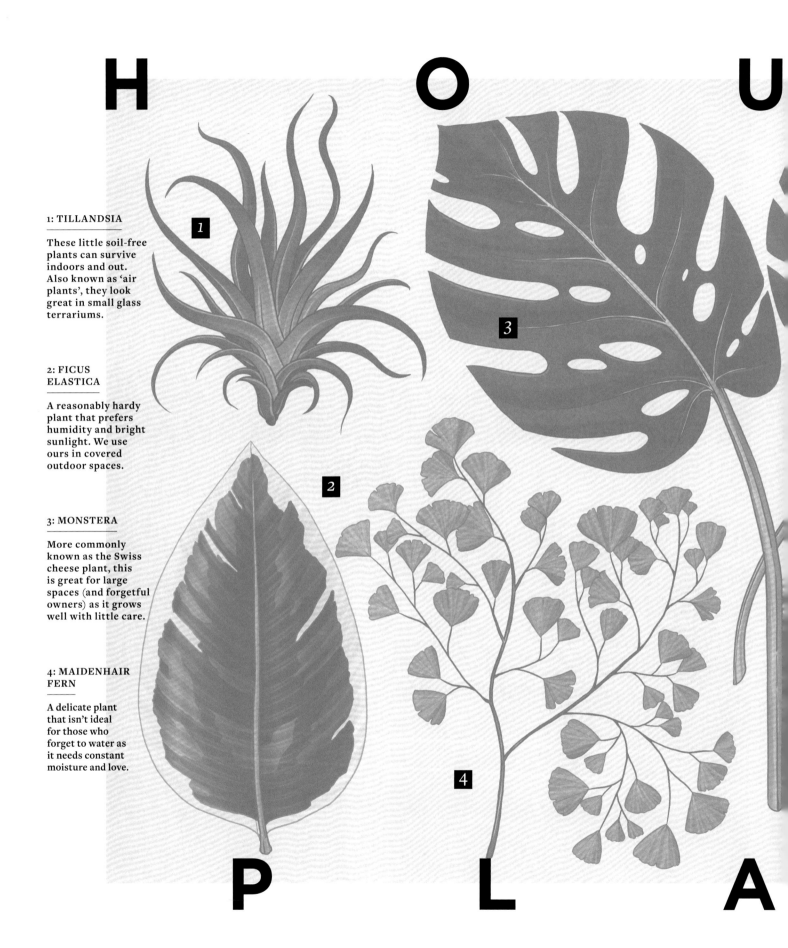

1: TILLANDSIA

These little soil-free plants can survive indoors and out. Also known as 'air plants', they look great in small glass terrariums.

2: FICUS ELASTICA

A reasonably hardy plant that prefers humidity and bright sunlight. We use ours in covered outdoor spaces.

3: MONSTERA

More commonly known as the Swiss cheese plant, this is great for large spaces (and forgetful owners) as it grows well with little care.

4: MAIDENHAIR FERN

A delicate plant that isn't ideal for those who forget to water as it needs constant moisture and love.

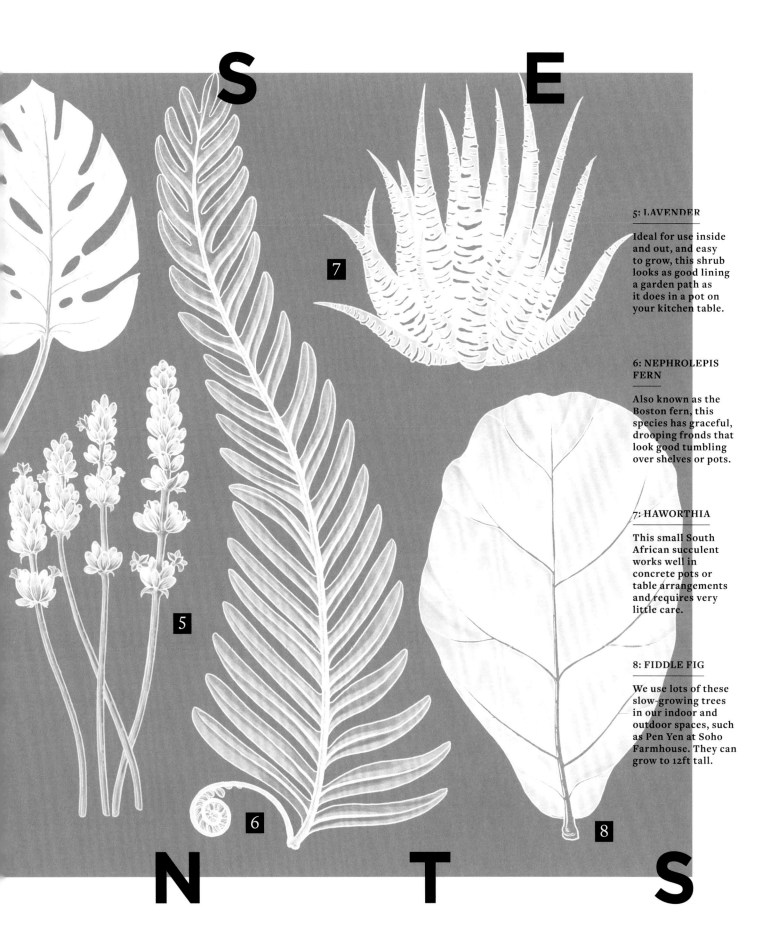

5: LAVENDER

Ideal for use inside and out, and easy to grow, this shrub looks as good lining a garden path as it does in a pot on your kitchen table.

6: NEPHROLEPIS FERN

Also known as the Boston fern, this species has graceful, drooping fronds that look good tumbling over shelves or pots.

7: HAWORTHIA

This small South African succulent works well in concrete pots or table arrangements and requires very little care.

8: FIDDLE FIG

We use lots of these slow-growing trees in our indoor and outdoor spaces, such as Pen Yen at Soho Farmhouse. They can grow to 12ft tall.

HOW TO CREATE A PICTURE WALL

We often hang our pictures salon-style so that they are clustered together. Here's how to do it at home...

FRAMING

Simple frames are best for contemporary work, and white, black and dark wood ones are all no-brainers. We often frame without a mount to create depth.

PALETTE

Artworks should complement the room, but not match. Choose a colour palette and then select different styles and media in that palette.

ART

Start with at least five pictures. Anything goes – photos, postcards, drawings, posters and pages from books will all work if they're framed well.

The Embassy Club,
Soho House Istanbul

LAYOUT

Artwork and pictures can be hung in symmetrical and ordered arrangements. The central picture should always be at eye level.

PLANNING

Place the standout piece first, then fill the surrounding wall space. Map out the pictures on the wall with Post-it notes or masking tape.

SOMETHING UNDERFOOT

Comfort comes high on our list of priorities. We use lots of rugs,
especially under beds, to add layers to a room and make padding
around barefoot warm and homely. We have several styles
we like to use around the Houses. Here are just a few.

KILIM RUGS

Flat-woven and hard-wearing, we use vintage and new kilim rugs of all sizes around the Houses, but particularly at Soho Farmhouse, where we lay them over chunky sisal for added texture. They lie perfectly flat, thanks to their lack of vertical weave, so are ideal for places with lots of footfall.

PERSIAN RUGS

Vintage Persian rugs are heavily patterned, but incredibly versatile. We use them in bedrooms, next to baths or under kitchen tables. We generally opt for Qashqai or Kazak varieties for their appealing geometric patterns and deep colours, but anything with character works well.

MOROCCAN RUGS

Fluffy, tactile and made in both neutral and bright colours, these traditional rugs are often the starting point when we come to design a room. One of the lofts in Soho House Berlin, pictured left, features a large tufted Moroccan rug and mid-century furniture.

JUTE AND SISAL RUGS

These rugs are tough, which is why we love them. They also have a natural, rustic charm that works perfectly as a counterpoint in urban settings. Sisal is particularly good for hallways and dining rooms. Softer jute rugs in Little Beach House Malibu add some texture to our outdoor spaces.

HOW TO PICK THE PERFECT RUG

With so many different styles, shapes and sizes, choosing a rug can feel overwhelming. Here are the six tricks we swear by when we're hunting for 'the one'.

1
—

Buy by colour, not by construction. Don't worry about the technical elements, such as whether it's hand-tied. Blues and reds are the most versatile and are a common colour scheme for the types of Persian rugs we like so much.

2
—

Borrow it before you buy it. Most good rug stores will let you do this. A rug can look completely different when it's in the light of your own home. Look at it from all angles. Depending on how it's woven, a rug can change in appearance from one side of a room to another.

3
—

The shorter the pile, the more hard-wearing the rug. Consider this when choosing rugs for spaces with lots of footfall, like hallways.

4
—

With thinner, flat-woven rugs, such as kilims, use a pad underneath to prevent it slipping. Ask your rug supplier or search for one online.

5
—

When buying a rug for beneath a dining table, allow for at least 2ft of rug on each end to accommodate the chairs. For example, if you have a 10ft table, you need a 14ft rug.

6
—

Always consider doorways. Most doors won't open over a rug, so choose your rug based on the size of your room with the doors open.

HOUSE TIP

Don't use chemicals to clean rugs. Dab with a 50/50 mix of water and white vinegar

A bedroom in the
Main House at
Babington House

Meet the Makers

LEWIS & WOOD

The British wallpaper and fabric producer works closely with artists
and designers in its Gloucestershire mill to transform hand-drawn patterns
into some of the wide-width wallpapers we've used in Babington House
and Soho House Barcelona. Established 20 years ago by textile printer
Stephen Lewis and interior designer Joanna Wood, Lewis & Wood is famous
for designs inspired by country living. Its eclectic collections include
original floral prints, as well as classic checks and stripes.

Opposite and top left:
Artist Flora Roberts hand-
paints the company's
Alhambra 100 wallpaper
design. Top right and
below: The Playroom and
the bar at Babington.

ALHAMBRA 100 BY FLORA ROBERTS FOR L

← TOP

One of the cabins
at Soho Farmhouse

LOUNGE IN A BEDROOM

BEDROOMS ARE PRIVATE PLACES FOR MORE THAN JUST SLEEP.
Adding a comfy sofa right next to your bed creates an extra space
in your house; a spot to read and relax with your favourite drink
before slinking off under the duvet. It's just another way
to escape the world.

A Big bedroom at
Soho House Chicago

Custom-made
wallpaper by
Pintura Studio
in the Velvet Room
at Ludlow House.

MAKING A HOUSE A HOME

THE EXCITEMENT OF MOVING INTO A NEW HOME
can easily be overtaken by logistical headaches. Over the years,
we've moved into 18 different Houses, all varying in age, shape and size,
and in vastly different locations, so we're familiar with the feeling
of 'where to start?' Vicky Charles, one of our interior designers
(who has been on site with every one of these moves), gives her
advice on how best to make your house feel like home...

Soho House Berlin

PLAN YOUR SPACE

It's easier to start with the simpler, flexible spaces of a house, and leave
more complicated rooms, such as kitchens and bathrooms, until you
are deeper into planning. Think of your bedroom as a calm corner
away from all the building work and general disarray.
Here's how we set about pulling one together.

1
—

First, choose the bed and plan its position in the room. Where it sits
will dictate the location of power outlets, wardrobes, rugs and almost
anything else. If you are installing new electrics, like light switches and
plug sockets, consider putting them within easy reach of the bed.

2
—

Plan your storage. Do you want built-in wardrobes or something more
flexible, say matching armoires? The former make better use of space,
but can look overpowering in smaller rooms. Weigh up the
pros and cons carefully.

3
—

A full renovation demands you commit to a furniture layout early on
and stick to it. While it's easy to shift around armchairs and rugs,
beds and wardrobes are the big items everything else needs
to work around.

4
—

Don't leave lighting to the last minute. Wall sconces require careful
electrical planning. The cable that supplies wall lights can come
from the top or the bottom of the sconce. Make sure you discuss the
lighting you want with your builders before they plaster the wall.

ADD SOME PERSONAL PIECES

We know how it goes. There are certain things that you just fall in love with. We found this lamp in a junk store in upstate New York. In the end, it led the way for an entire scheme, and its unusual colours were reflected in the wallpaper of the Parlor at Ludlow House.

UNUSUAL FINDS

We liked how the fabric on these chairs by Clarence House looks like a Kandinsky painting. The quirky, vintage colours and patterns of the cloth became the inspiration for the look and feel of the whole rooftop restaurant at Ludlow House.

ORIGINAL ART

We work with lots of artists from around the world. At Little Beach House Malibu (pictured below), we installed a floor-to-ceiling art wall in the stairway, featuring the work of Matt Connors and Jonathan Yeo. But good art doesn't have to be rare or expensive. A lot of paintings for our bedrooms are discovered at markets, thrift shops and even on eBay.

A cabin at Soho Farmhouse features a custom-made mohair sofa with kilim-covered seats and cushions.

IT'S OK TO
CHANGE YOUR MIND

Sometimes you just have to try things out and see what works.
Mistakes have happened in every House we've designed. But risks often
pay off and make a room unique. When we got this bright-yellow velvet
sofa into position at Soho House West Hollywood, it was clear the
white walls behind it were just not working. 'We changed it to rich teal
instead,' says Nick Jones. 'It feels like a commitment, but paint is
the easiest and cheapest thing to change in a room. Start by painting
a square on the wall and keep it there for a while until you have taken in
the impact it has on the space. Listen to your gut feeling and go with it.'

MIX AND MATCH

Mixing patterns and colours can enliven a space. 'Over-thinking colour schemes makes a house feel predictable and boring,' says interior designer Vicky Charles. 'With our bars and living rooms, we keep it free and creative. We want the design to influence people's behaviour and say, "You can let loose in here. Have a good time."'

MAKE A COMMITMENT

Fall in love with one thing, no matter how outlandish, and the rest will fall into place. 'This sofa was covered in a very bright and tricky fabric we had been waiting to use forever. Everything else just had to work around it,' says Vicky.

'We often find that what doesn't make sense on paper can actually work brilliantly in action. In order to put your stamp on a home, it's important to be brave and try new things'

NICK JONES

CARVING OUT A CORNER

Creating one quiet and organised corner can really help
you stay sane when the rest of the house is in chaos. Whether
it's a corner of shelves arranged neatly or a nook with an armchair
to run away to, maintaining some sort of order is important.

Soho House Chicago

NIGHT

OUR HOUSES GO THROUGH TRANSITIONS
all day long, but for most of our members, it's the
evening hours they really look forward to. Live
music, well mixed drinks and tasty food are just some
of the things we aim to get right, night after night.

Fancy Farm, on the
mezzanine level
of the Main Barn
at Soho Farmhouse.

DINNER AT NAVA

LOCATED ON THE 13TH FLOOR OF THE BUILDING
that's home to Soho House West Hollywood, Nava has panoramic
views of The Valley and a California meets the Middle East inspired
menu. The design – fresh, clean-lined, relaxed – reflects the food.

WATERCRESS AND CHICKPEA SOUP

Serves 4 | Prep: 10 mins | Cook: 25 mins (V)

INGREDIENTS

1 tablespoon olive oil
1 medium brown onion, peeled and finely sliced
2 garlic cloves, peeled and finely sliced
10g/⅖oz ginger, peeled and finely sliced
200g/7oz chickpeas
200g/7oz watercress
100g/3½oz spinach leaves, washed
600ml/1 pint vegetable stock
Salt and black pepper, to taste
Watercress, paprika and crème fraîche, to serve

METHOD

Heat a large pan with a little olive oil and add the onion. Season
with salt and cook until light golden in colour. Then add the garlic
and ginger, cooking slowly.

Add the chickpeas, watercress, spinach and stock and cover.
Cook for around 5 minutes or until the leaves have wilted.

Pour the soup into a blender and blitz until smooth. For a very
smooth soup, use a sieve. Add freshly ground pepper and salt to season.

We like to serve with a fresh sprig of watercress, a few whole chickpeas,
a pinch of paprika, a little olive oil and a dollop of crème fraîche.

HOUSE
TIP

Add a pinch of sugar
at the seasoning stage
if the soup tastes
too peppery

BUTTERNUT SQUASH WITH SLOW-COOKED ONIONS AND PISTACHIO PESTO

Serves 4 | Prep: 10 mins | Cook: 1 hr 30 mins Ⓥ

INGREDIENTS

1 butternut or acorn squash, cut into wedges, seeds removed
3 red onions, peeled and finely sliced
250ml/9fl oz white balsamic vinegar
2 teaspoons honey
3 sprigs of fresh thyme, leaves picked
Pomegranate seeds, crushed pistachios and feta cheese, to serve

FOR THE PISTACHIO PESTO:

50g/1¾oz pistachios
35g/1¼oz grated pecorino or hard goat's cheese
Extra virgin olive oil
25g/¾oz fresh coriander
50g/1½oz fresh parsley
25g/¾oz fresh dill
25g/¾oz fresh mint
Juice of 1 lemon, to taste
Salt and pepper

METHOD

Preheat the oven to 180°C/350°F/gas mark 4. Place the squash in
a roasting tin, drizzle with a little olive oil and roast for 50-60 minutes.

For the pesto, blitz the pistachios and cheese in a food processor with
75ml/2½fl oz extra virgin olive oil, then add the herbs and lemon juice,
season and pulse quickly.

Set the oven to a temperature of 160°C/320°F/gas mark 3. To slow cook the
onions, cover with balsamic vinegar and a drizzle of honey, then add the thyme.
Wrap the onions in foil for 30 minutes, then open slightly and continue cooking
for a further 30-45 minutes. This prevents the onions from drying out. Place the
squash and onions on a plate or serving dish, then cover with the pesto.
Scatter over the pomegranate seeds, pistachios and feta cheese to serve.

CAULIFLOWER SALAD
WITH POMEGRANATE & ALMONDS

Serves 4 | Prep: 30 mins ♡

INGREDIENTS

1 medium white cauliflower, finely chopped
4 large spring onions, finely sliced
250g/9oz cooked freekeh (see below)
2 ribs celery, finely sliced
10g/⅓oz parsley, 10g/⅓oz mint and
10g/⅓oz dill leaves, all finely chopped
1 pomegranate, seeds only
30g/1oz flaked almonds, toasted
Salt and white pepper, to taste

FOR THE DRESSING:

1 garlic clove, peeled
4 sprigs fresh thyme, leaves picked
15ml/2½ teaspoons pomegranate molasses
40ml/1⅖fl oz red wine vinegar
55ml/2fl oz extra virgin olive oil
Salt and freshly cracked white pepper

Pound the garlic and thyme in a pestle and mortar, then place in a bowl.
Add the pomegranate molasses, then whisk in the red wine vinegar and oil.
Season with salt and white pepper.

FOR THE FREEKEH:

450g/16oz freekeh
700ml/1½ pints water

In a sieve, rinse the freekeh grain to remove excess starch. Combine the water and freekeh in an oven-safe casserole dish that will allow room for the grain to expand to double the volume. Cover with tin foil and bake in the oven at 180°C/350°F/gas mark 4 for 45 minutes to 1 hour, until the grain is tender. Leave to cool, or store in the fridge to use the next day.

METHOD

Combine all the ingredients in a large bowl, then season with salt and white pepper. Mix in the desired amount of dressing to your taste. We like to serve garnished with celery leaves (the yellow sweet leaves taken from inside the bunch) and a sprinkle of pomegranate seeds.

HOUSE
TIP

Place the
pomegranate flesh
side down, then tap
with a rolling pin
to remove seeds

DECONSTRUCTED CHEESECAKE WITH LEMON & PISTACHIO

Serves 6-8 | Prep: 20 mins | Cook: 20 mins Ⓥ

INGREDIENTS

500g/1lb 2oz full fat cream cheese
150g/5oz feta
Zest of 3 lemons
125g/4½oz icing sugar, sifted
125g/4½oz honey
1½ teaspoons rose water
500ml/17fl oz double cream
100g/3½oz shop-bought
kadaif filo
40g/1½oz salted butter, melted
1 teaspoon caster sugar

FOR THE CRUMBLE:

280g/9½oz pistachios
90g/3⅕oz plain flour
40g/1½oz soft unsalted butter
145g/4⅘oz caster sugar
1 teaspoon salt
¼ teaspoon vanilla extract
1 egg
Pinch of salt

Blitz the nuts and flour in a food processor
until you have fine crumbs, then set aside.

Cream the butter, sugar, salt and vanilla extract
in an electric mixer. Add the egg, mixing well
and scraping the sides of the bowl as you go.
Add the flour and nut mixture until combined.

Spread the dough out and pat evenly until it is
3mm thick. Bake at 180°C/350°F/gas mark 4 for
20 minutes until golden. Allow to cool, then
roughly crumble using your hands or a fork.

METHOD

In an electric mixer, combine the cream cheese,
feta and lemon zest and beat until smooth.
Add the icing sugar and honey and mix until
combined. Turn the mixer to its lowest speed
and pour in the rose water and double cream.
When the mixture thickens, tip it into a plastic
bowl, cover with cling film and set aside.

Place the filo on a parchment-lined baking
tray, loosen the shreds and lay flat to cover
the tray. Mix the melted butter with the sugar.
Once dissolved and slightly cooled, pour over
the filo, fully coating it. Take a pair of scissors,
and cut the filo to make four even 12cm/4½in
squares. Bake at 180°C/350°F/gas mark 4 for
12-15 minutes until golden.

To serve, layer the filo, then the cream cheese
mixture, and top with a sprinkling of crumble.
We like to add a few rose petals and a side of
poached quince to the plate.

HALVAH SUNDAE WITH SESAME ICE CREAM & SALTED CARAMEL SAUCE

Serves 4 | Prep: 20 mins | Cook: 40 mins (V)

INGREDIENTS

ICE CREAM:

440ml/15fl oz double cream
440ml/15fl oz whole milk
2 vanilla pods
$\frac{1}{2}$ teaspoon salt
80g/2$\frac{3}{4}$oz sesame seeds, toasted
6 egg yolks
170g/6oz caster sugar

SALTED CARAMEL SAUCE:

180ml/5$\frac{3}{4}$fl oz double cream
1 teaspoon vanilla extract
170g/6oz granulated sugar
55g/1$\frac{4}{5}$oz glucose
55ml/1$\frac{3}{4}$fl oz water
50g/1$\frac{3}{4}$oz butter
1 teaspoon salt, to taste

SESAME BRITTLE:

55g/1$\frac{4}{5}$oz butter
55g/1$\frac{4}{5}$oz granulated sugar
20g/$\frac{4}{5}$oz glucose
20ml/4 teaspoons milk
120g/4oz sesame seeds
Pinch of salt

METHOD

FOR THE ICE CREAM:
Bring the cream, milk and vanilla pods to the boil, take off the heat and add the toasted sesame seeds and salt. Set aside for 1 hour to infuse. In a separate bowl, whisk the egg yolks with the sugar. Sieve the milk and cream mixture to remove the seeds and vanilla pods. Place back on the heat and bring back to the boil. Pour over the yolk and sugar mixture, whisking vigorously at the same time. Freeze in the ice cream maker.

FOR THE SAUCE:
Heat the cream and vanilla extract and set aside. Caramelise the sugar, glucose and water until amber. Remove from the heat and whisk in the warm cream mixture slowly and, once combined, whisk in the butter until emulsified, then add the salt. Allow 15-20 minutes to cool. If making the sauce in advance, store in an airtight container, or keep in the fridge overnight if using the next day.

FOR THE BRITTLE:
We recommend making this in advance. Melt the butter, sugar, glucose and milk, but don't let the mixture boil. Remove from the heat, and stir in the sesame seeds and salt. Place the mixture on a tray lined with non-stick baking paper, and flatten. Top with another sheet of paper, and flatten as thin as you can using a rolling pin. Carefully peel off the top sheet. Bake in the oven at 160°C/320°F/gas mark 3 for 7-10 minutes until golden. Remove, allow to cool, then break into pieces.

To serve, combine a little bit of everything with a few wild berries.

WINDING
DOWN

The Luckman,
Soho House
West Hollywood

HOUSE TIP

For a chilled drink without ice, place the glass in the freezer for a few hours before serving

BITTER JEAN

INGREDIENTS

60ml/2fl oz single malt whisky
15ml/½fl oz crème de cassis
22ml/¾fl oz Carpano Antica Formula sweet vermouth
10 dashes Angostura bitters
2 bar spoons peated whisky or similar
2 maraschino cherries, to serve

METHOD

Stir all the ingredients together with ice and strain into a vintage glass.
Serve with two maraschino cherries on a cocktail stick.

Soho House
West Hollywood

Soho House
76 Dean Street

THE PENICILINA

INGREDIENTS

50ml/1¾fl oz blanco tequila
25ml/¾fl oz lemon juice
15ml/½fl oz ginger syrup
10ml/⅓fl oz honey water
mezcal spray
Crystallised ginger, to serve

METHOD

Shake the ingredients together and
strain over ice. Serve in a cut-crystal
tumbler and garnish with a few cubes of
crystallised ginger on a cocktail stick.

RUBBING
IS RACING

INGREDIENTS

60ml/2fl oz blanco tequila
30ml/1fl oz fresh lime juice
15ml/½fl oz Giffard
Banane du Brésil
15ml/½fl oz ginger syrup
1 egg white
3 dashes Angostura bitters

METHOD

Measure all the ingredients into
a cocktail shaker and dry shake
(no ice) to emulsify the egg white.
Add ice then shake again. Strain
into a sour glass and top with the
Angostura bitters. Run a tooth
pick through the middle of them to
create hearts in the foam and serve.

Ludlow House

Nava, Soho House
West Hollywood

GRASSHOPPER
REVIVED

INGREDIENTS

30ml/1fl oz crème de menthe
30ml/1fl oz crème de cacao
30ml/1fl oz single cream
7ml/¼fl oz Fernet-Branca
Crushed ice, to serve
Mint sprig, to serve

METHOD

Measure all the ingredients into
a shaker, then shake and double strain
into a rocks glass filled with the crushed
ice. Garnish with mint and serve.

HOUSE TIP

For impact, garnish
with a smouldering
cinnamon stick
resting on the rim

SMOKED RUSTY NAIL

INGREDIENTS

**25ml/¾fl oz Island single malt
25ml/¾fl oz blended scotch
infused with 4 cinnamon sticks
25ml/¾fl oz Drambuie
15ml/½fl oz lapsang syrup**

FOR LAPSANG SYRUP:

**50g/1½oz lapsang loose tea
500ml/18fl oz water,
heated to 95°C/203°F
200g/7oz sugar**

Allow the tea to steep in the water for
3-4 minutes. Remove the leaves, then stir
in the sugar until it dissolves. Store any
excess in the fridge for future use.

METHOD

Stir all the ingredients with ice and
strain over rocks into a rocks glass.

Soho Farmhouse

The Club Bar,
Soho House Chicago

The terrace
at Duckedup,
Ludlow House

EVENINGS AT LUDLOW

OUR NEWEST NEW YORK CLUB HAS BEEN DESIGNED
with late nights in mind. Live music plays each week in the
Velvet Room, so named because the club resides on the same street
where The Velvet Underground's John Cale and Lou Reed once shared
an apartment. There are three bars, a screening room, a roof-terrace
restaurant and plenty of dark nooks in which to while the night away.

HOUSE
TIP

Install a central
dimmer switch to create
relaxed light levels
in darker spaces

INTO THE NIGHT

'We embrace rooms that are naturally dark,' says Nick Jones. 'In the
Parlor at Ludlow House, we enhanced the cosiness by adding dark walls.
Low lighting keeps things intimate and grown up. In a good way.'

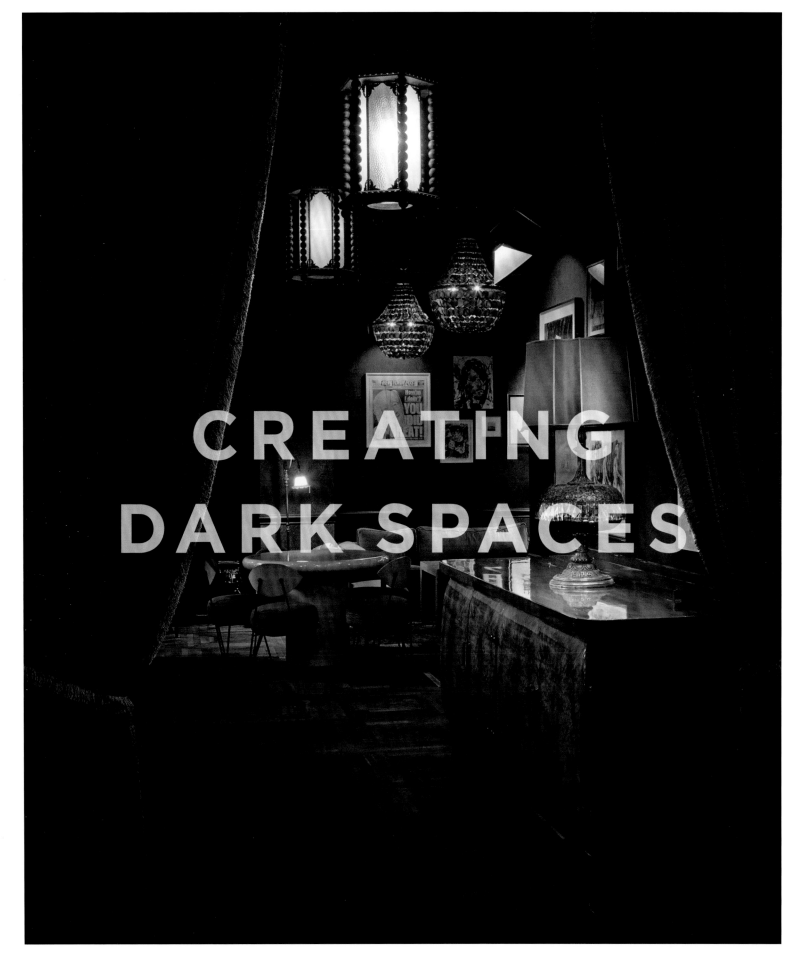

CREATING DARK SPACES

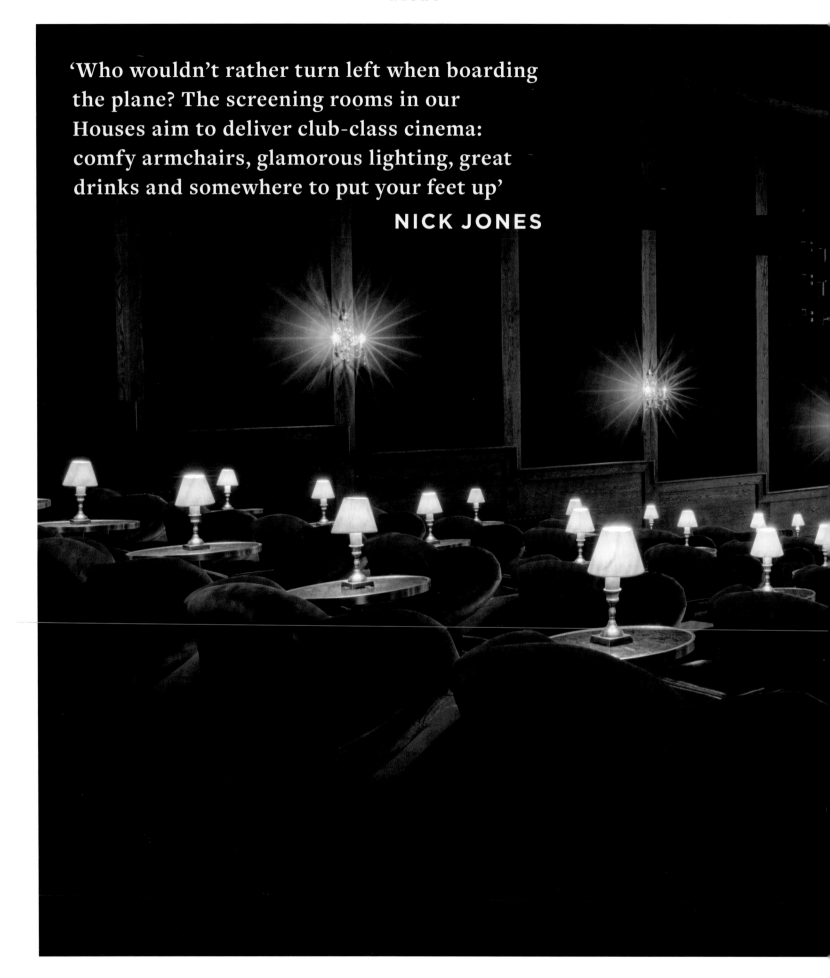

'Who wouldn't rather turn left when boarding the plane? The screening rooms in our Houses aim to deliver club-class cinema: comfy armchairs, glamorous lighting, great drinks and somewhere to put your feet up'

NICK JONES

The screening room
at Soho Farmhouse

SCREENING ROOMS THE SOHO HOUSE WAY

Cinema is make-believe. A bigger, bolder and mostly better version of life. We try to make our little cinemas like that, too. Here's how we go about it.

1
—

All Soho House screening rooms have the best in technology, from a 10m/32ft wall-to-wall screen to Dolby Atmos immersive sound.

2
—

We go to great lengths to ensure every seat gives maximum comfort and a good view of the screen.

3
—

Low-level lamp lighting and heavy velvet screen curtains give a nod to the glory days of Hollywood cinema.

4
—

We avoid serving food in our screening rooms – even popcorn. We prefer our cinema-goers to enjoy a meal before or after the film, so there's nothing to distract them or fellow viewers.

5
—

When it comes to drinks, however, we're all for it. A chilled glass of chablis or a reviving negroni can make a good screening into a great one.

Cheers and enjoy the movie.

The screening room at
Soho House 76 Dean Street

THE IMPORTANCE
OF GOOD GLASSWARE

A drink is a treat. A reward.
A celebration. And the right
glass is as crucial as the
correct ingredients. There is
something about drinking from
crystal that elevates the merely
enjoyable to the simply superb.

A RANGE OF STYLES

A well-stocked glass cupboard is essential when entertaining. If you can, keep a range of styles in your drinks cabinet, from copper mugs to classic cut-glass highballs.

A SENSE OF CEREMONY

There's something glamorous about the coupe glass. Invented in England in 1663 for drinking champagne, we love them for their high-polished elegance, and use them to serve cocktails, too.

CREATING YOUR OWN DRINKS TROLLEY

All our bedroom guests enjoy their own cocktail station. Some are housed in cabinets, others take the shape of a vintage drinks trolley. Here's how to recreate one at home.

SPIRITS

The basis of any good bar is the spirits. Our trolleys are often stocked with Grey Goose vodka, Bombay Sapphire or Cotswold gin, Bacardi Carta Blanca rum, Jose Cuervo tequila and Jack Daniel's whiskey.

FRUIT

Oranges, lemons and limes should never be in short supply; you can use them in simple spirit mixes, cocktails and soft drinks.

MIXERS AND MODIFIERS

Tonic and soda water are essentials. Campari, orange curaçao or triple sec and St-Germain are all useful to have to hand.

GLASSWARE

Good crystal can really enhance the pleasure of a drink. We recommend stocking at least two cut-crystal highballs, two cut-crystal tumblers, two champagne coupes and two white wine glasses.

TOOLS

A small, sharp knife, peeler, bottle opener, cocktail shaker, bar spoon and a small marble chopping board will come in useful. An ice bucket and tongs complete the set.

EXTRAS

Agave syrup is a mild sweetener made from the same plant as tequila: it blends well in lots of cocktails and isn't too sweet. Angostura bitters are also useful; just a drop can transform the most basic of drinks.

Top: original 1970s Kalmar glass chandeliers in the Drawing Room in Soho House Chicago. Below: a custom-made Swarovski chandelier in Soho House New York (left); a vintage chandelier in Fancy Farm at Soho Farmhouse (right).

SOURCING
CHANDELIERS

The wrong lighting can ruin a room and spoil an evening.
On the other hand, flattering low-key lighting is transformative
on the space and the experience. Chandeliers help bring a sense
of decoration and polish to even the simplest of rooms. 'We prefer
to see the bare bones of the building,' says interior designer
Vicky Charles. 'Adding a chandelier is a lovely contrast
– a piece of precious jewellery hanging in the room.'

**HOUSE
TIP**

Clean your crystal
using a lint-free cloth
sprayed with a solution
of 1 cup vinegar and
3 cups warm water

A BRIEF HISTORY OF THE CHANDELIER

Over the years, we've sourced hundreds of antique chandeliers. From mid-century Italian to American ballroom, they have become key features in our bedrooms, bars and bathrooms. Here, we chart their ornate origins.

1300

The first chandeliers date back to the 1300s and were simple in design, often made from a wooden cross with small spikes to hold candles. These were mostly used in medieval churches and abbeys.

1434

More complex brass designs were developed as chandeliers and entered the palaces and homes of the wealthy. In 1434 Flemish painter Jan van Eyck produced one of the earliest paintings of a chandelier in *The Arnolfini Portrait*.

1676

English glassmaker George Ravenscroft introduced lead glass to the world of lighting in 1676. Far easier to cut than rock crystal, this soon became the preferred material for chandeliers and, as designs improved, the crystal chandelier became fashionable.

1736

The word chandelier dates back to 1736, originating from the French word for candle (*chandelle*). Neoclassical designs and chandeliers blown from Venetian Murano glass were both popular in the 1700s.

1879

After the invention of gas lighting, many candle-lit chandeliers were converted. The design of modern chandeliers slowly changed after the electric light bulb was introduced in 1879.

1910

The chandelier crash is a key scene in Gaston Leroux's novel *The Phantom of the Opera*. Andrew Lloyd Webber's musical adaptation uses a one-tonne replica of the Paris Opera House chandelier, made with more than 6,000 beads.

2010

The largest chandelier in the world, designed by Scottish lighting designer Beau McClellan, took two years to make, and is 5.8m tall, 12.5m wide and 38.5m long.

A chandelier at
Soho House Chicago

RESTORING BUILDINGS

SOHO HOUSE ISTANBUL

A GRAND 19TH-CENTURY PALAZZO IN THE HEART OF
the ancient city's Beyoğlu district, our House in Istanbul merges
old and new to form 87 bedrooms, a spa, gym and a traditional
hamam. It was originally built in 1830 as a residence for a wealthy
Genoese family, before being turned into Istanbul's
first American consulate.

The teams took more than two years to restore and renovate
Palazzo Corpi, including the main entrance, staircases and frescoes.

'THE MORNING ROOM features an original parquet floor and wood-panelled doors. We added vintage furniture, a large velvet sofa and antique lamps.'
James Waterworth, interior designer

The Main Bar (pictured opposite) features one of the largest frescoes in the House and took a team of experts more than 18 months to restore. The wrought-iron and marble staircase dates back to the original building.

AROUND
THE FIRE

There's no substitute for a beautiful fireplace.
At Farmhouse, each cabin features a wood-burning
stove (pictured below). In Little Beach House Malibu,
we put one pride of place in the Dining Room (opposite).

FINISHING TOUCHES

'We always try to reflect the palette of a room with our final details,' says interior designer Vicky Charles. The Velvet Room in Ludlow House features an antique marble fireplace dressed with plain white ceramics. Lilac velvet chairs sit on a vintage 1940s Chinese rug and above, an original painting by Tracey Emin is lit with a fibreglass pendant lamp by Constance Guisset for Petite Friture.

Soho House Berlin

TURNING IN FOR THE NIGHT

GOING TO BED SHOULD BE A PLEASURE RATHER
than a chore. At turn-down, we lower the lights, plump the
pillows and make sure things are just right so you can enjoy
that last nightcap, late-night snack or soak in the tub.

'The hotel room turn-down
is one of the best bits
about staying away.
I love it so much, we're
now doing it at home'

NICK JONES

Turn-down lighting sets
the mood at Shoreditch
Rooms Club Row, London.

THE BEDROOMS TO BOOK

All our bedrooms are unique but some have that extra wow factor. Here, interior designer James Waterworth chooses three of his favourites.

MEDIUM BEDROOM, SOHO HOUSE BARCELONA

'This is eclectic and spacious, yet cosy and comfortable. The curved iron bed, deep red rug and floral motifs on the curtains all make a nod to traditional Catalan style.'

BIGGER BEDROOM, DEAN STREET TOWNHOUSE

'In line with the building, this bedroom was given a late Georgian aesthetic. The four-poster bed was made specially and makes staying here feel like an event in itself.'

MEDIUM PLUS BEDROOM, SOHO HOUSE ISTANBUL

'This is in the House's modern annexe. The carved doors were made to reflect a similar antique pair we found in the original 19th-century palazzo.'

SHOREDITCH ROOMS CLUB ROW

'Shoreditch has an edge to it,' says James. 'We needed to reflect that with the design of the bedrooms. As such, they are fun, playful and have lots of colour.'

'We always pay attention to headboards. Staying in one of our beds should feel like an indulgent experience, and being able to sit up and relax in bed is all part of that'

JAMES WATERWORTH

This page: Soho Farmhouse (top), Babington House. Opposite: Shoreditch Rooms Club Row.

Farmyard Up,
Soho Farmhouse

GETTING A GOOD NIGHT'S SLEEP

As life gets busier, a full night's rest can seem hard to come by. Here are five tips we encourage around the Houses to help you on your way.

1
—

Remember that alcohol can impede your ability to sleep all the way through the night. Keep hydrated before you hit the hay by drinking a carton of electrolyte-rich coconut water.

2
—

Take a bath to get you in the zone. Add a few drops of aromatherapy oil, such as lavender or mandarin, to help yourself calm down and de-stress.

3
—

We like to keep certain comforts close at hand. In all our bedrooms, we provide an eye mask, a pair of ear plugs and a hot water bottle with a cashmere cover to ensure you get the best night's rest possible.

4
—

Avoid dealing with big decisions before you go to bed. Sleep on it. A good rest can give you a whole new perspective by morning.

5
—

Keep a notebook by the bed. Writing down your to-do list helps clear your mind and prepare you for the next day.

CHOOSING CURTAINS

They are one of the biggest investments you make when designing a room, so it's important to get them right. 'Sometimes it's nice when curtains hang a touch too long,' says interior designer Siobahn O'Flaherty. 'A crumple on the floor adds to that lived-in feel and looks a bit more luxurious.'

KEEPING OUT THE LIGHT

How to balance style and practicality when it comes to your curtains.

1
—

If you are investing in good fabric, get your curtains made by professionals to avoid expensive mistakes. Be specific when requesting the type of pleats and finishes you want – different curtain-makers use different terminology.

2
—

If you are using patterned fabrics, buy more than you need because the repeat pattern will need to be matched when the widths are stitched together.

3
—

The curtains at Soho Farmhouse are purposely simple: weighty linens and heavy cottons in shades of grey and stone with no tie-backs. These will work well anywhere.

4
—

Try to reflect the property with your choice of curtain. If the building is Georgian, like Babington House and 76 Dean Street, rich curtains with trims and full pelmets look great.

5
—

Interline the curtains with a plain blackout fabric to keep out the light. Make sure the curtain and tracks come back beyond the window, so no light creeps in at the edges. The same applies to blinds.

6
—

We always use a double pole with our curtains. The simple (and cheaper) back track carries the voiles, which are useful for allowing light in during the day, while still maintaining privacy. The front pole can be more ornate (and expensive).

A Main House bedroom at Babington House features richly patterned curtains with tasselled leading edges and rustic linen voiles.

SKINCARE BY NIGHT

At Cowshed, we take our evening routine pretty seriously, which is why we created Sleepy Cow, a range of products featuring calming ingredients and essential oils to help you sleep, and wake up feeling and looking refreshed. Here are a few ways we like to get some rest.

1
—

Encourage your body to relax with a soak in the tub. Bathing helps open pores, slough away dead skin and prepare your body for sleep. Sleepy Cow Calming Bath Salts have a blend of melissa and lemon myrtle essential oils, designed to relieve tension.

2
—

Use our Knackered Cow Bath & Body Oil either in the bath water or as a massage oil after your soak. Infused with calming lavender and uplifting eucalyptus essential oils, it's just the ticket for tired muscles (and minds).

3
—

Start your evening routine by cleansing and exfoliating your face before applying our Chamomile Refreshing Toner. Before you head to bed, apply Rose Replenishing Night Cream and Jasmine Toning Eye Balm to your face. Both are designed to help your skin look firmer and reduce the appearance of fine lines the next day.

4
—

Your skin regenerates at night, so taking certain supplements before bed may actually improve it. Biotin, vitamin C and omega-3 fatty acids are all good for both skin and hair health and get to work while your body is resting.

RESTORING BUILDINGS

LUDLOW HOUSE

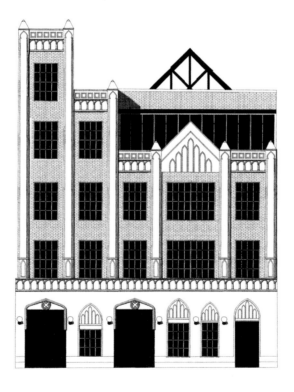

OPENED IN JUNE 2016, LUDLOW HOUSE OCCUPIES
a former funeral parlour and gold leaf factory on New York's
Lower East Side. Our team fell in love with the tiled façade and
gothic feel of the building. The unusual colour palette we used inside
was inspired by the bottle-green tiles of the original bathroom.

The large double doors at the entrance feature antique brass handles. The Soho House design team spent months scouring antiques markets and fairs in New York to find the perfect vintage pieces.

THE PARLOR IS LOCATED on the ground floor, and features a wallpapered ceiling, shell chandeliers, reclaimed wood flooring and an open log fire.

The lighting in the steel staircase is from a 1930s department store in Chicago, while
Lou's Kitchen & Bar features a tiled floor to give it the feeling of a classic American kitchen.

THE
NIGHT
CAFE

LARDER ESSENTIALS

Whether you're after late-night comfort food or just getting in
as the sun is rising, keep these staples in stock at home and you'll
always be able to rustle something up.

IN THE CUPBOARD

Canned tuna: sustainably sourced
Baked beans: we love the original Heinz
Spaghetti: straightforward dried pasta
Bread: white or sourdough

FROM THE FRIDGE/FREEZER

Eggs: free range or organic
Cheese: a strong cheddar
Ham: medium to thick-cut, never processed
Bacon: streaky for extra flavour
Fish fingers: frozen, fresh, or homemade with panko crumbs for extra crispiness
Peas: frozen are great for their sweetness
Butter: makes everything taste better

CONDIMENTS

Mayonnaise: always buy the best quality you can find
Ketchup: it's got to be Heinz
Mustard: Maille Dijon is our favourite
Worcestershire sauce: for extra tang or, if you can find it,
we also like Henderson's Relish from Sheffield

TUNA MELT

Serves 2 | Prep: 5 mins | Cook: 6 mins

INGREDIENTS

160g/5½oz tuna from a can, drained
40g/1½oz mayonnaise
Salt and pepper
2 slices bread (white, brown or seeded, to your taste)
80g/2¾oz cheddar, thinly sliced

METHOD

Preheat the grill to high. Mix the drained tuna with the mayonnaise,
and season with a little salt and pepper.

Lay the bread on a flat, parchment-lined baking tray and place under the grill to lightly
toast on both sides. Remove from the oven, then divide the tuna mixture between `
the two slices of bread. Top each with cheese and place back on the tray, then
return to cook under the grill until the cheese is bubbling.

Season with a further sprinkling of pepper before serving.

HOUSE TIP

For an extra kick,
add a dash of
Tabasco sauce
to serve

FISH FINGER SANDWICH

Serves 2 | Prep: 2 mins | Cook: 15 mins

INGREDIENTS

6 fish fingers
4 slices white bread
Unsalted butter (we use Lurpak) and tomato ketchup, to serve

METHOD

Preheat the oven to 200°C/400°F/gas mark 6. Place the fish fingers on a tray and bake for 15 minutes until golden and crispy.

Meanwhile, spread the slices of bread with a generous amount of butter.

For each sandwich, place three fish fingers between two slices of bread, and add ketchup to serve.

HOUSE TIP

We recommend using a basic, good-quality sliced white bread, like Kingsmill

WELSH RAREBIT

Serves 2 | Prep: 10 mins | Cook: 5 mins Ⓥ

INGREDIENTS

20ml/4 teaspoons Worcestershire sauce, plus a dash
to serve (or Henderson's Relish if you have it)
20g/¾oz unsalted butter, cubed, plus 20g/¾oz for frying
10g/⅖oz mustard (Maille Dijon is our favourite)
130g/4½oz cheddar, grated
2 egg yolks
Salt and freshly milled black pepper
2 slices bread (to your taste; we like to use sourdough)

METHOD

Preheat the grill. Meanwhile, create your rarebit mixture. Place the
Worcestershire sauce in a small saucepan and bring to the boil.
Remove the pan from the heat, then whisk in the butter and the mustard.

Add the cheddar and place the pan over a low heat. Be careful not to let
the cheese get too hot – you may need to move the pan on and off the
hob at times to get the right temperature. Stir until melted, then remove
from the heat once more, and whisk in the egg yolks. Season generously
with freshly milled black pepper.

Place a non-stick frying pan over a medium heat. Once warm,
add 1-2 tablespoons of butter. When the butter begins to bubble,
add the two pieces of sourdough and cook until golden. Turn the slices
over, and spoon the rarebit mixture over each toasted side. Leave on
the hob for 1 minute before placing under the grill for 1-2 minutes,
or until the mixture browns.

Season with salt and pepper to your taste. We like to serve with
an extra dash of Worcestershire sauce or Henderson's Relish.

HOUSE
TIP

For a rich flavour, add
125ml/4½fl oz stout to
the pan. Reduce to a
syrup, before making
the rarebit mixture

**HOUSE
TIP**

Mix 1 tsp of Dijon
mustard with 1 tbsp
of mayonnaise and
spread inside
each sandwich

CHEESE AND HAM TOASTIE

Serves 2 | Prep: 5 mins | Cook: 7 mins

INGREDIENTS

4 slices bread (white, brown or seeded, to your taste)
4 slices ham
100g/3½oz cheddar, thinly sliced
(Montgomery or Westcombe are our favourites)
Salt and pepper
Unsalted butter

METHOD

Preheat the oven to 180°C/350°F/gas mark 4.

Place two slices of bread on a board, and divide the ham between each one,
then add the cheese and sprinkle with salt and pepper. Cover with the remaining
slices of bread and spread a thin layer of butter on top.

Heat a non-stick frying pan over a medium heat. Place the sandwiches in the pan, buttered side
facing down. Spread a thin layer of butter over the outside slice of bread now facing up in the pan.
Cook for 2 minutes until the bread is golden brown – check using a pallete knife
and cook for longer if need be.

Once golden, turn the sandwiches over and cook for a further 2 minutes. Transfer onto
a parchment-lined baking tray and place in the oven for 3 minutes. Once the cheese has fully
melted, remove from the oven, then slice into fingers and serve.

SPAGHETTI CARBONARA

Serves 2 | Prep: 10 mins | Cook: 10 mins

INGREDIENTS

10ml/⅓fl oz olive oil
160g/5⅖oz thick-cut bacon, diced
200g/7oz good-quality dried spaghetti
1 small shallot, finely chopped
1 clove garlic, peeled and chopped
Salt and freshly milled black pepper
100g/3½oz Parmesan, finely grated, plus 10g/⅓oz to serve
2 egg yolks

METHOD

Heat the olive oil in a sauté pan over a medium temperature. Add the bacon, fry until golden and crispy, then remove and set aside in a dish. Keep the bacon fat in the pan and place back on the hob. Turn the heat down to low.

Meanwhile, bring a saucepan of salted water to the boil for the spaghetti. Cook the pasta as directed by the instructions on the packet.

When the sauté pan has cooled down slightly, add the shallot and garlic, and cook gently. Add 10 turns of black pepper and then 50ml/1¾fl oz of the water from the pasta. Set the pan to one side. Once the pasta is nearly ready, place the sauté pan back on the hob and bring to the boil. Drain the pasta, reserving some of the cooking water.

Pour the cooked pasta into the sauté pan and stir well. Top with the grated Parmesan and remove from the heat. If the pasta is looking dry, add more of the reserved cooking water. Keep stirring until all the cheese has melted. Now mix in the cooked bacon, stir once more and finally add the two egg yolks stirring quickly to prevent them from cooking. At this stage, make sure you don't get the pan too hot otherwise the cheese sauce can split and the eggs may scramble. Once mixed together, serve with salt and pepper to taste.

HOUSE TIP

To add colour and a fresh flavour, cook some frozen peas and throw in before serving

LAST NIGHT'S SHEPHERD'S PIE

Serves 2 | Prep: 2 mins | Cook: 5-10 mins

INGREDIENTS

Last night's shepherd's pie, chilled in the fridge
2 eggs
1 can of baked beans

METHOD

Shepherd's pie is one of those dishes that always tastes better
the next day. And everything tastes better with a fried egg.

Remove the shepherd's pie from the fridge and cut out two square-shaped,
individual portions. Place in a pan and reheat on the hob until piping
hot all the way through.

Serve each portion with a good-sized helping of baked beans
and the aforementioned fried egg.

HOUSE TIP

The same sides work just as well with last night's fish pie

ONE FOR THE ROAD

CHELSEA'S DAGGER

INGREDIENTS

45ml/1½fl oz pisco
15ml/½fl oz cherry brandy
25ml/¾fl oz grapefruit juice
15ml/½fl oz lime juice
15ml/½fl oz cinnamon syrup (see recipe below)
5ml/1 bar spoon of cherry syrup
Orange peel and a cherry, to serve

CINNAMON SYRUP

100g/3½oz caster sugar
100ml/3½fl oz water
4 cinnamon sticks

Dissolve the caster sugar and water in a pan over a low heat. Add four cinnamon sticks and leave to infuse for one hour, then remove. Store any remaining syrup in the fridge.

METHOD

Put the ingredients in a cocktail shaker with ice. Shake vigorously to break up the syrups. Double strain into a footed Collins glass.

Add crushed ice, and garnish with a slice of orange peel and a cherry.

LATE-NIGHT LISTENING

Music is a subtle but important detail when it comes to creating atmosphere
in the Houses. When the evening is winding down and you're looking
to relax with friends, drink in hand, here are some albums to match the mood.

J.J. CALE – NATURALLY (1972)

Cale's debut album from the 1970s has all the makings
of a true, laid-back country-rock record. It's a classic.

KHRUANGBIN – THE UNIVERSE SMILES UPON YOU (2015)

Making soul and psychedelia feel modern, the Texas trio's
debut album is reminiscent of a Quentin Tarantino soundtrack.

SINKANE – MEAN LOVE (2014)

Slow pop music with wide-ranging influences and soulful
touches make for a cool, smooth combination.

DAVID BOWIE – ZIGGY STARDUST (1972)

Bowie's fifth studio album, and one of the greatest concept records ever made.

BIBIO – A MINERAL LOVE (2016)

Soft but still lively, Bibio's seventh album continues
to set the pace for the folktronica genre.

Soho House Berlin

The Roof,
Soho House Chicago

PHOTOGRAPHERS

Adam Gichie, Alicia Clarke, Andrew Burton,
Britt Willoughby Dyer, Can Köroğlu, Chris Terry,
Chris Tubbs, Damian Russell, Dave Burk,
Dylan + Jeni, Emily Kelly, Engin Aydeniz,
Gesi Schilling, Jake Curtis, Jodie Harrison,
John Stoffer, Lawrence Watson, Malcolm Menzies,
Mark Seelen, Mehmet Ateş, Mike Rosenthal,
Montse Garriga Grau, Nathan Michael,
Sarah-Louise Marks, Sean Myers,
Tim Evan-Cook, Tom Mannion,
and Light Project Photography

ILLUSTRATORS

Katie Scott and Thibaud Herem

CREDITS

Produced and edited by Jodie Harrison
Written by Jodie Harrison, Lucy Quick,
and Alex Hawkins
Designed by Giles Arbery at Wild Billy & Crazy Dave

SPECIAL THANKS TO

Vicky Charles, James Waterworth, Kirsty Young,
Siobahn O'Flaherty, Chelsea Nelson, Kellyann Hee,
Scarlett Supple, Linda Boronkay, Aurelie Coulibaly,
Ruth Costello, Tim Knowles, Billie Edington,
Chelsea Lavin, Mandy Kean, Annie Brooks,
Peter Chipchase, Tanya Nathan, Ed Victor,
Rachel Hales, Nazrene Hanif, Tom Collins,
Ronnie Bonetti, Neil Smith, Nicholas Wilber,
Dave Giles, Eric Estrella, Tom Kerr, Casey Sorenson,
Anna Greenland, Jo Whitfield-Jones,
Anastasia Koutsioukis, Niklas Juli, Collette Lyons,
Daisy England, Dominique Bellas, and Yasmin Angileri

SOHO HOUSE